Flush the Fear

A DIY Guide for Eliminating Fear, Anxiety &

Negative Crap from Your Life

By

Beth Allen

HIP Chicks Press

©2020 Beth Allen
All rights reserved.
Published by HIP Chicks Press
ISBN 978-0-578-63893-5

Cover photograph
www.kararaudenbushphotography.com

Back cover photograph
www.daniellesoloffphotography

Interior photographs
www.mattallenproductions.com

Cover design
Donna FitzGerald

DEDICATION

To Ken, the man who showed me the power of unconditional love.

I shall love you for a thousand years.

PRAISE FOR FLUSH THE FEAR

This book really struck a chord with me. You can live your life wallowing in the negative or you can be empowered to create the life you want, flush all of the past away and use the lessons to move into the present stronger. Beth details her own story and her work with women to show others how they can be better to themselves and more connected with others. Her playful and humorous analogies make it an easy read while addressing some serious issues along the way. By reading this book you will realize that you cannot wait for people or circumstances to change around you. You have the power to build a better world for yourself.

Jennifer Lynn Robinson - CEO Purposeful Networking

Ah, the sweet relief of letting go! In her new book, *Flush the Fear - A DIY Guide to Eliminating Fear, Anxiety and Negative Crap from Your Life*, Beth Allen teaches readers to own the negativity we almost nurture--because it's what we know--and then flush it away like the ugly mess it is. With warmth, authenticity and humor, she tells the challenging tale of life with a mother unable to accept her and the work needed to rebuild her mother-less world. Using her skills as a DIY expert, Beth provides a toolbox of exercises, tips and tricks to retrain your brain, moving you towards emotional wholeness and health. Read this book and get ready to let go of the yuck!

Mary Fran Bontempo - Speaker, Author: *The 15 Minute Master,* maryfranbontempo.com, Co-Founder, BrilliantlyResilient.net

This is an amazing book! Beth Allen provides all the tools you need to move forward and take charge of your life. I love her story and I love the concept. I will definitely be using my new tools in everyday life.

Brigitte Rogers - Writer, Founder BLifeToday.com and Talent Producer at NFL Films.

For a book that starts out on the potty, it's an absolutely delightful read! What more can I say? This book will be in my bathroom and on my coffee table. Well done, Beth..."Flush" will help so many people on many different ways through joy and tenacity. I'm a fan.

Marilyn Russell - Radio Host WOGL 98.1

Table of Contents

INTRODUCTION

All of a sudden it hits you—that overwhelming sense of discomfort. Something inside you just needs to come out. You try hard not to focus on it, but the pressure intensifies. You shift your body in a lame attempt to find some reprieve. You imagine the satisfaction you'd feel if you could just let it go. Yet, the more you think about it, the more uncomfortable you feel. A few deep breaths will help you cope, or so you think.

Hastily you park the car and burst through your front door with anxiety running high.

There it is. The porcelain potty!

You can now let go of your angst.

You can now let go of your shit! Literally and figuratively.

Thank you, toilet, for being there when we need you most!

Thank you, toilet, for inspiring this book!

And thank you for helping us let it GO!

. . . .

Why the Toilet?

Frankly, I am fond of the toilet, also known as the Potty, the John, or the Crapper (affectionately named after its inventor Thomas Crapper). Whatever *you* call it, we all have a unique relationship with this commonplace household object. And unless you are reading this deep in the wilderness, I bet you used the facilities at least once today already! But my fondness for the toilet goes way beyond the ordinary usage. I have had a lifetime of interesting moments involving the toilet, so many moments that it inspired this book.

It started when I was three years old and the flower girl in my aunt's wedding. I went to use the bathroom after the ceremony, determined to do it all by myself (a personality trait that has only grown with age) and I tragically dropped the skirt of my full-length yellow lace gown straight down into the toilet. It was ruined. Thank God it was after the ceremony and the photos because my beautiful little princess gown was soaked, thoroughly soaked with toilet water. I spent the rest of the day running around the reception in my undershirt and slip. I've never heard the end of that wardrobe malfunction. Every one of my family members remembers it but me!

Fast forward to my adult life and the toilet is a simple, sturdy reminder of other defining roles in my life:

- Potty Training — As a mom raising three sons, I have spent many an hour around the toilet — either cleaning one or encouraging my boys to develop precision aim with a handful of Cheerios.

- Potty Reports — During my days as a registered nurse, I had a degree that deemed me an expert in assessing patients' health by the characteristics of their, you know, stuff! I had the distinct pleasure of measuring and documenting the quality and quantity of what my patients left behind — pun intended — and what a "dooty" it was!

- Potty Whisperer — As a licensed contractor and handywoman, I'll fiddle in the toilet tank, fixing that super-annoying flapper or wayward chain. My friends call me the Potty Queen! You really ought to open the lid and see what goes on in there. It's fascinating.

- Potty Prose — Despite my many hands-on experiences with toilets, never in my wildest dreams did I imagine that I would find a message of personal growth in the bottom of a toilet bowl. But I did and I believe you can, too.

How did I arrive at a place in life where I wrote a book about a toilet? It's been 30 years in the making; I just didn't know it until now.

In the last ten years, I went from being a stay-at-home mom wrangling my little men at the park to being a tool-wielding woman teaching other women how to nail a stud (in the wall that is) all while creating a business from nothing. This was not in the plan, but like many women with school-age children, I found myself wanting something that sparked my sense of purpose aside from my role as mom. When my boys were little, I wanted nothing more than that. My guys were the center of my world and I theirs. But as they grew more independent, I knew I needed to develop myself.

You see, I saw the downside of losing yourself in motherhood. I watched my mother lose herself when I was a teenager and ultimately battle years of mental health issues. Her struggles led to an emotional breakdown and a 27-year estrangement from me; her choice, not mine. With full clarity and intention, I could not and would not let history repeat itself with my own family. I needed to be myself. I needed to pursue my own dreams and have ambitions independent of my children and husband. I was ready to discover what my next move would be. I found my life's purpose. Oddly enough, it involves a chicken and a toilet.

My purpose is helping women to be smart, capable, and confident homeowners. The goal — to save them money, time, and aggravation taking care of the biggest investment of their lives. I built a business around teaching women do-it-yourself skills. I call it HIP Chicks — the Home Improvement Project Chicks — with a super cute chicken logo of my sidekick Henrietta. My tagline says it all: "I Teach Women How to Screw... and Hammer, too!" Sassy and bold, but all in good humor!

The most amazing thing happened in the process of teaching women about screwdrivers, clogs, and tripped circuits. I realized that these self-reliant home-repair skills were helping them to be more resourceful and independent in general. I would see the "I got this" look in their eyes. They were developing life skills along with their DIY skills. They felt powerful with power tools in hand and more empowered as individuals. Not only can my HIP Chicks walk into any Home Depot ready and able to tackle their projects, but their can-do attitude also spills over into other aspects of their world. They feel more capable and confident as partners, as moms, and as individuals — a beautiful yet unexpected outcome from fixing a toilet flapper. I began to think more deeply about how this self-reliance impacts the most important parts of life — home, health, and family.

So, I pondered. How could I use this home-repair angle to help women tackle their real-life issues? Why not put as much energy into our self-improvement as we do into our home improvements? I use my platform of home improvement to craft stories and lessons that help us "fix" ourselves. Now I know we are not necessarily "broken," but we all can benefit from continued improvements. I built my message around experiences in relationships, parenting, work, and self-care to create *Flush the Fear*, a DIY guide for self-improvement!

Self-improvement can mean many things to many people — changing unhealthy behaviors, embracing new beginnings, or moving past the past! No matter what it is for you; it often requires rolling up your sleeves and getting down and dirty to make things better. It's just part of the process.

I must admit that when I read self-help or relationship books, I think they are a bit preachy. It is the nature of the beast when people share their stories. It's the "Hello, people, this worked for me so you should do it, too" approach. My goal is to share my personal perspective on motherhood, work, marriage, and angst. I have worked through a lot of crap myself and if I can spare you some of the stress I experienced, it will give my pain some purpose.

My goal is to empower you to live your best life because you can learn to set anxiety and fear aside. This book can't remove all the stress in your life. No book can. I do believe I can help you take small, simple daily actions to let go of the crap that brings you down. I wrote this book for the women out there who are in the trenches of motherhood, trying to do it all and be it all for everyone in their life. I wrote it for the daughters who might not understand the crazy behavior of their moms, but will someday. I wrote it for the men who walk beside us, helping us navigate this mother-daughter relationship in the best way possible.

Flush the Fear moves through the process of looking at fear, anxiety, and the negative crap in our lives with a new perspective. It is a journey of personal development, yours and mine, as we create a life that is filled with more joy, more peace, and more moments that take our breath away. Think of it as a Do-It-Yourself Guide for Building a Smarter, More Capable, and More Confident YOU!

Part One: Flushing Fear

Toilets and Fear?
Yes, We Are Going There

Toilets and Fear. What a ridiculous correlation, you say? Just indulge me for a minute. This porcelain inanimate object bolted to the bathroom floor has been known to bring on a lot of anxiety. Potties can be the center of some crazy unpleasantness. Remember those college party hangovers driving the porcelain bus, begging the porcelain god to make it all stop? Or those nasty GI bugs that leave you feeling so bad you don't know if you should sit or kneel? And you parents out there, you have dealt with those potty-training disasters that required latex gloves and Lysol!

Now, imagine this hypothetical yet very plausible scenario. You are at the Millers' New Year's Eve party. Thirty of your friends and neighbors are all gathered in the kitchen. It's the party of the year. Cocktails and appetizers are aplenty. You can't help but indulge in a little too much of Maria's Famous Taco Dip, Then suddenly it hits… that overwhelming urge. You have to do… a Number Two. There is no waiting. You must go and go now! The only accessible bathroom is, of course, right off the kitchen, a.k.a. party central. You go into the bathroom to do your business, hoping no one knows what you are doing. You flush and as you turn to wash your hands, panic sets in. You see that the water in the bowl is not going down. Your stuff is coming back up; it's quickly approaching the rim! The water level is rising faster than your heart rate. Your hands are cool and clammy. The only thing in that bathroom that is *flushing* is your FACE. You pray, "Dear God in Heaven, don't let it overflow, don't spill over," but... it does just that. Can you see it now? That walk of shame through the kitchen to find Mrs. Miller to ask her for a plunger, paper towels, and some disinfectant. You fear you will be forever known as The Party Pooper! Oh, the horror.

A little melodramatic for sure, but you must admit that sometimes the toilet is a bit scary. You germaphobes get it. The anxiety you feel while using a public restroom can be crippling — the germs, the smells! Pooping outside the privacy of your own bathroom is difficult for many. The thing is, you are not alone. There is a legitimate psychological diagnosis for this type of anxiety. It's called parcopresis — the fear of having a bowel movement in public restrooms. I kid you not!

Speaking of the kids, for them this idea of toilet phobia is very real. Toddlers are often afraid to climb up on that cold seat, set their bare bum over that dark hole and *let go of their stuff*. Where do you think the psychological term anal-retentive came from? Freud developed a theory about personalities based on a child's early experience using the toilet. In his time, having only limited access to a toilet or chamber pot caused a "wait." He hypothesized that if toilet training was a stressful process, the child developed an inclination to hold back and retain his or her stuff, out of a need for control. In modern times, anal-retentive people are described as needing control, order, and cleanliness. Freud would say the inner child is still trying to manage the environment and having a hard time letting go of things.

Sometimes this tendency lingers into adulthood. As adults, we too are afraid to let go of our "stuff." Not necessarily body waste, but rather the negative things in our heads; the issues we just can't seem to move past. Perhaps it is the same stuff we've carried around since we were kids, too often it is something traumatic. Sometimes it is recent life drama that has us bound up! No matter how long you have been holding on to your stuff, I call that habit of fixating on our unpleasant moments, "emotional constipation." We hold onto the past so tightly that it hurts, physically and emotionally. And the longer we hold it to it, the more it stinks!

No worries though. Even when you are emotionally constipated, the toilet can be a vessel to help you pass the stuff that has you stopped up. It's not just there for you to sit your ass on as you scroll through Instagram. It can help you purge emotionally. We'll get to that exercise later.

To Flush the Fear from our lives, hypothetically speaking, we need the tools to do so. I'm going to share the tools that got me through the pain of my family separation. It was my traumatic moment. Holding onto my sanity didn't happen without working at it. I want to help you step back from the everyday nonsense that we get caught up in and make a deliberate, conscious choice to let go of your shit! Because living with fear and anxiety is just too hard and it sucks the life out of us.

Scientific studies have confirmed this. Living with anxiety, fear, and depression is physically hurting us. It is hurting our kids, too. Consider this finding from Harvard Health Publishing:

> Anxiety has been implicated in several chronic physical
> illnesses, including heart disease, chronic respiratory disorders,
> and gastrointestinal conditions. When people with these disorders

have untreated anxiety, the disease itself is more difficult to treat, their physical symptoms often become worse, and in some cases they die sooner.

These dark things affect our sleep, weight, immunity, digestion, relationships, and work. They show up in the way we love others and most often in the ways we treat ourselves. Living in this state of angst is holding us back from, dare I say it, being happy. When was the last time you felt truly happy and joyful? Don't YOU deserve to be happy every day? YES! Yes, you do.

Before we can flush our fears, we need to take a deep look at where fear is coming from and how it shows up to wreak havoc on our lives.

Where Does The Crap Come From?

We all have a story, one filled with good, not so good, and sadly, some downright bad experiences. It is from those unhappy moments that our current crap begins to grow, like unwanted grey hairs creeping slowly into and onto our heads. Wouldn't it be great if we could rub out the root of our fears as easily as we do our greys? Unfortunately, a $5 box of "Nice and Easy" hair dye won't cover up what truly burdens us. Those unforgettable events in our past may fade but they leave scars. Whether it was a one-time incident or years of angst, most of us have had something painful in our past that follows us around like toilet paper stuck to our shoe.

I've got mine and it runs deep. I've been carrying it for 30 years. I totally understand that no one really wants to revisit the painful moments or admit how often the past shows up in our present. Most of the time, we just don't recognize it happening, but we need to own it and identify it if we're going to have a chance of flushing it out. I'll share more of my story in Chapter 3.

Suffice it to say, we all have our shit to sift through. It is unpleasant. Frankly, it stinks. No one is exempt and owning up to it is nothing to be ashamed about. It's quite the opposite, in fact. It is freeing.

Our fears and anxieties run deep. Sadly, many of them are rooted in our childhood; seeds of fear that were sown by experiences with loneliness, shame, or pain. Just like Pavlov's animal research showed a correlation between stimuli and consequence, we humans react to the memories of our past experiences, the good and the bad. We avoid things that leave us with a negative consequence or bad feeling, though some of us are drawn to the negative trigger because we find odd comfort in the pain. Many people often think that they deserve the pain because somewhere along the way someone told them so. As much as we think we have a handle on the past, or even try to avoid it, those memories linger and show up unexpectedly in the here and now.

Maybe the memory of dad packing up his things and moving out during a divorce leaves you struggling with abandonment issues. It keeps you from committing to that awesome guy because deep inside you expect he will leave you, too. Why wouldn't he? Your own dad didn't stick around for you. Not true, of course, but we can believe just about anything if we tell it to ourselves often enough.

Perhaps as a teenager, you hid your brother's alcohol addiction from your friends. You wouldn't invite friends over because they might see his drunken rants or violent outbursts. Years later, you keep friends at bay because you built a pretty high wall around yourself where you hide with the shame that still lingers.

Have you struggled with body image? Did someone call you fat when you were young? Maybe that person was in your family. Perhaps a slight comment just rolled off their lips like butter but hit you like a steamroller. You have spent years riding the weight-loss roller coaster, perhaps even reaching your goal, but deep down you still feel incredibly insecure about your body. Words matter, and sadly they seed themselves in the most vulnerable spaces in your head until they fester like weeds in a garden overtaking everything around them.

Or are you the type who works relentlessly to be the best at everything? You stress yourself out trying to be perfect because if you are perfect, MAYBE, just maybe, your mom will finally show you the unconditional love and acceptance you craved as a child and never got.

Does any of that sound familiar? The last one creeps back into my head too often. But whatever it was that affected your upbringing, you are not alone. We have all had our ugly family memories, from a painful divorce, neglect or poverty to an exasperating vacation, a tense holiday or birthday party gone wrong. Unfortunately, our family relationships are often the biggest source of pain and angst. Family dysfunction touches everyone. I always say, no one puts the FUN in dys*fun*ction like family!

On a very serious note — these issues from the past can create very real consequences in the present. Abuse, rape, and abandonment leave deep psychological scars. When trauma is not treated with the right help and guidance, addiction, eating disorders, violence, and self-harm can ensue. You may not be able to manage the pain alone, especially if it is leading you to unhealthy behaviors. Professional help is never something to shy away from or be embarrassed about. It can be lifesaving. Therapists help you do the stinky work of sorting your shit! If we don't do that work, fear and insecurity will keep us rooted in pain, failed expectations, negative mindset, and unhappy memories.

What the Hell Are You Afraid of?

"Lions and tigers and bears! Oh My!" We all know that line from The *Wizard of Oz* as Dorothy and friends navigated the Enchanted Forest. But what's on your list? From things that go bump in the night to airplanes and snakes, we all have fears, irrational ones and sometimes very sane ones that drive our actions for good and bad reasons. Fear often drives our motives!

There is much research on fear and its power over us. Many studies over the last decade outline the predominant fears that affect Americans; #1 was public speaking, followed by flying, spiders and, of course, the perennial list-topper, death. These are all justifiable causes of anxiety and panic attacks, except the spider thing. I don't get that one. Just get a shoe, and the problem is solved! But the rest of the list is reasonable cause for angst.

Fast forward to 2020 and you can see that fear has taken a different twist. It's not just spiders and snakes and clowns that make us tremble. Our fears go deeper into our psyche. More recent studies and articles about fear share that there are fewer people with phobia-centered fears and more with psychological-based fears. Today, psychologists are citing more Americans are struggling with: disappointment, death, poverty, rejection, and failure.

Read them again. Disappointment. Death. Poverty. Rejection. Failure.

That's one heck of a list. I think I'd rather deal with lions, tigers and bears! These are concerns that impact our relationships, our work, and our health. These are real everyday issues, not trivial things like the occasional spider. Worries about putting food on the table. Worries about your family rejecting you because you tell them you are gay. Worries about your cancer coming back. This is real angst. Real fear.

Let's delve a little deeper into this list and think about where these fears are rooted in the past.

Disappointment – When my kids were little, I used to say the line. "You get what you get and don't get upset." Well, that line may be fine for discouraging a toddler's meltdown over getting the red popsicle versus the orange, but in our adult life our let-downs are more complicated. Our fear of disappointment is often tied to feelings of unworthiness. We doubt we will ever have X, so we subconsciously behave in ways that don't support the goal. When we miss the mark, we rationalize that we didn't deserve it and nothing good ever happens to us anyway. We can't be disappointed if we never reach for more. It's self-sabotage.

Often we have trouble separating ourselves from situations. We can't accept the fact that we were not selected for a promotion because another person was simply better suited. We take things personally, not pragmatically. We feel that promotion slipped through our fingers because we were not good enough, not smart enough, etc. When we repeatedly look at life's outcomes through a mirror, it is easy to make let-downs purely about us. I hate to tell you this, but I will anyway. It's not always about you!

Life is full of disappointments, from the creamy brown ice cream that isn't chocolate but coffee flavored, to not getting into your top-choice college. We all have expectations for how we'd like life to unfold, but the universe has other plans sometimes. But if we imagine the world saying "not yet" instead of "not ever," we would be better able to cope with our disappointments now and even find the balls to put ourselves out there again until the hoped-for thing happens. Learn from the experience of feeling disappointed, don't fear it.

Death – The word itself just brings angst to most of us, but for some people the fear of death can be crippling. Thanatophobia, as it is called, can grow from several thought processes – fear of pain in the process of dying, worries about leaving loved ones behind, fear of eternal punishment, and more. Many people report anxiety around funerals and cemeteries because they had a disturbing or unsettling experience in childhood with the death of a loved one. Imagine as a child being forced to go up to a dead parent or grandparent for a viewing. This ritual is terrifying for some kids and even adults, too. These moments, when not handled in healthy ways, can have lasting effects on how we view the death of others and ultimately ourselves. Negative attitudes are often passed through generations and cultures. We can change the narrative with open conversation and support during mourning periods and grief rituals. Death is going to happen, so why not talk about it and ease the sting when it does?

Poverty – This is a very real fear for so many. I saw this growing up. My parents worried about, fought about, and cried about money. How little we had, where it was going, and where it was coming from were their constant concerns. Like many Americans, they were responsible working-class people who found it hard to make ends meet. Money was always a source of angst and stress. I still carry negative emotions about money even though I am not as vulnerable financially as my parents were. Worrying about how to provide a roof, a meal, and an education for your kids is nothing new and it is destructive. Not being able to provide for yourself and others challenges your self-worth, your self-reliance, and your sense of purpose. This deep kind of worry can leave you in a constant state of fight or flight while you juggle multiple jobs, tend to kids, and skip self care. Money woes and a lack of financial sense can drive poor decisions as stress keeps you on edge and the cycle repeats itself. Understanding these money-driven fears will empower you to have a healthier relationship with your finances and your future. Do you carry unresolved money issues? You are not alone and can work through them for a more stable financial future. Remember, the power to get past any issue starts with recognizing that it's an issue. Then you need to find an advisor to help you make changes.

Failure – It is simply understood as not succeeding at accomplishing a task or reaching a goal. At times, we all fail to get something done or get it done correctly, but the fear of failure is problematic when we view *ourselves* as failures. According to psychologist Guy Winch, PhD, in Psychology Today, "People who have a fear of failure are motivated to avoid failing not because they cannot manage the basic emotions of disappointment, anger, and frustration that accompany such experiences but because failing *also* makes them feel deep shame."

A sense of shame and uselessness can take over when we can't separate the failed tasks from ourselves. That shame eats away at our ego and self-worth. Those feelings keep us from trying to tackle new things. We tell ourselves that we can't accomplish "X" because we didn't achieve these other things. We create a self-fulfilling prophecy where we just expect to fail and the self-sabotage begins. Stop the cycle by setting attainable goals. Check things off the list so you see progress and stop seeing yourself as a do-nothing, but as a doer.

Rejection – This one runs deep for me. I could not express the emotion any better than this excerpt from John Amodeo, PhD (2014) in *Psychology Today*: "The fear of rejection is one of our deepest human fears. Biologically wired with a longing to belong, we fear being seen in a critical way. We're anxious about the prospect of being cut off, demeaned, or isolated. We fear being alone."

At 21, I was cut off from my family. I challenged the status quo with my mother and her unhealthy behavior. For drawing a line in the sand regarding how our family was interacting, I was told that I abandoned her. I have spent my whole adult life questioning my self-worth and how I could possibly be lovable if my own mother did not love me anymore. I know I am not the only one who has ever felt this way. Whether you were rejected by a friend, a sibling, a partner, or a parent, the pain lingers in your soul and seeps into every relationship you will ever have. The fear of rejection follows us to job interviews, dates, business meetings, and social situations. It turns us into people pleasers, enslaved to others' opinions and it keeps us from being who we are meant to be. It can leave us feeling unloved, unlovable and unwanted. It doesn't have to be this way.

So many of us are carrying these bundles of worry and pain upon our backs. We can't always find easy or quick solutions to ease them, but we can try to learn ways to handle the stress they bring on. We can do little things to change the way we look at anxiety and worry. Very often the things that have us stuck are not so much the actual stimuli but the negative energy and emotions that stem from them: a combination of painful memories, self-deprecating thoughts, and self-hate. We can't change what happened to us in the past, but we can change how we cope in the future. We can learn how to move past it.

My life changed when I began to say no to my fear of rejection.

An Empty Tank Of Emotion

For 27 years, I have struggled with feeling unlovable, unworthy, and rejected. When I was 20, my seemingly happy life unraveled. I became permanently estranged from my parents. It was not a situation I desired, nor one I saw coming. Being rejected by the people who are supposed to love you more than anyone in the world cuts deeply, very deeply. It leaves you empty.

My relationship with both of my parents was kind and caring throughout my childhood. We had a simple life with not much money, but I have fond memories of family, food, and laughter. In my late teens, the family dynamic began to change. Our family sailed into a perfect storm. The storm was the collision of two women entering two very different stages of life. My mom and I were both facing changes beyond our control. One of us felt doors closing in, while the other saw them opening wide. Our roles in life were being redefined in unexpected yet tumultuous ways. Neither of us was prepared for this storm nor its aftermath.

Growing up, my mom was my role model. She taught me to fix things. I remember climbing scaffolding at 10 years old to help her wallpaper the stairwell. My mom and I tackled lots of crazy projects together and my dad just let us do our thing. In our house, she ruled the roost and Dad always said, "It's her way or the highway." I later came to understand how true that was. Few people ever told her no.

When I was 17, my mom had an emergency hysterectomy. She had ignored symptoms of a fibroid tumor for a long time until she hemorrhaged. Post-op she faced the sudden onset of menopause; the "change" brought about major changes in her personality as her hormones shifted. It happens to many women. Sadly, after the hysterectomy, she refused hormone treatments and follow-up care. Her emotional state began to disintegrate. She had always been a worrier, but during this period her anxiety escalated. She worried about everything, tried to control everything, and feared everything. She had outrageous visions of car accidents or abductions. When my dad went to the doctor for mild chest discomfort, she paced the house saying we'd be okay on my nursing salary if something happened to him. One winter, Mom was convinced she had lung cancer, not bronchitis, but wouldn't go to the doctor. She didn't want to know if it was going to be bad news. Paranoia drove her behavior and her behavior was driving me away.

My older siblings were out of the house, being 9 and 10 years older. I was the center of Mom's world. We were close and spent a lot of time together, but my life was expanding around friends, work, and college. As my world grew bigger, hers seemed to grow smaller. She was not prepared for me needing her less… and for her needing me more. The eye of the storm was over us. Resentment, narcissism, and anger took over the woman I had known. Dark days followed.

I was living at home while working towards a bachelor's degree in nursing, trying to juggle school, work, friends, and my mom. Her emotional needs grew daily as her anxiety and depression deepened. I tried to play therapist and had to do it alone. While my dad was the optimist in my life, he had no clue how to deal with my mom. He was unwilling to challenge her. I will never forget the night she and I had a big blow up. Amid tears and screaming, dad stopped me in the hall outside my room. He said, "Kid, I love you, but if I have to choose her or you. I will choose her. You'll have to figure it out on your own."

Imagine the emptiness of hearing your own parents tell you that you are not their priority.

I was crushed. The guy I thought had my back, didn't. I was alone.

Dad said I would manage on my own. I guess he was right. But at the time it all seemed so unbearable and hopeless. This woman I admired and looked up to was now my biggest antagonist. I could do nothing right. She claimed that I never gave her enough of my time and that my view of the world was all wrong. In my head, I knew that was not true but holding onto reality was tough in the midst of blow-out fights filled with twisted interpretations, manipulated emotions, and at times, fast-moving projectiles. Branded in my memories are a few physical alterations that I never could have imagined I would ever have with my mom.

I shared the reality of what was happening at home with just a few friends; not even my brother and sister truly knew how bad things were. I wanted to spare them. They were both newlyweds and starting their own lives. I thought I could handle it. I was wrong.

The worst days were when the threats of suicide began; they were only aimed in my direction. It usually involved threats of pills or of sticking a rag up the tailpipe of the car. My mother would not say anything about such a grave act in front of my dad. It was just a quiet dance we shared. I would get home from work at midnight, wondering if I would quietly slip into my bed, encounter another screaming match, or find the unimaginable. This went on for months. I begged her to see a doctor, a priest, or a therapist—anyone who could help her manage her anger and fear and pain. I bought her a bestselling self-help book and watched her throw it across my room one night in total rebuke. I was a 20-year-old girl trying to fix someone she loved, someone who didn't want to be fixed.

I was alone, worn out, and desperate to change the dynamic. I felt helpless and hopeless. I then began to consider an out for myself. Some nights on the drive home from the hospital, I would ponder which telephone pole on Route 611 South would be the best one to wrap my car around—a quick way to end my despair and hers, too.

Fortunately, life intervened in an unexpected way. One night at work, an older physician pulled me aside. He was concerned about my work performance, because I seemed very distracted. His fatherly kindness broke me down and in the quiet of an empty exam room, I spilled my guts. He showed such insight and compassion for both my mom's perspective and mine. He encouraged me to seek professional help, and to push her to get some, too. He shared two deeply insightful things. Things that changed my life.

Dr. A. told me that I was not responsible for my mom's happiness. What? I wasn't? Really? How could that be? I grew up in a house where when mom was off, everyone had to work to calm her. We all accepted responsibility for whatever made her unhappy and we tried to fix it. No one had ever told me that I, Beth Ann, was not responsible for how she felt or how she reacted to life's challenges. That one single idea was so freeing. Now of course, that idea doesn't mean that we are not responsible for the pain our unkind behavior brings to others. If you hurt someone, you are responsible for that. But no one had told me that I was not responsible for my mom's mental health. I was carrying that burden and, God, was it heavy.

He also shared with me this one simple statement. <u>I deserved unconditional love</u>. WOW. Unconditional. No strings attached. Free from manipulation and obligation. Free from biting criticism and violence. Loved even when I made a mistake or disappointed. Loved without expectation or reciprocation. Loved despite my imperfections. Really? Did such a thing exist? Did I really deserve that?

Unconditional love. He made me want to find it, want to have it. Later that week, I began seeing a therapist and I again begged my parents to go with me so we could get our relationship back on track. But like many in her generation, Mom would not air our dirty laundry. No one was to know our business. In her mind, therapists turn you against your family. I knew keeping silent would destroy me. I went alone. I was simply trying to save myself.

A few weeks after starting therapy, I made the most courageous decision of my life. I moved out of my parents' home. With a hard-earned $7,000 to my name, I bought a used car and some thrift store furniture, and rented a small apartment. Yes, maybe that seems like a lot of money back then, but I also had a final year of college tuition on my plate. I had no umbrella to cover me, no safety net to catch me. When I left home, it was very clear that I would not be welcomed back. My mom felt I had abandoned her. I couldn't help but feel like my parents had abandoned me.

I believe that was Mom's greatest fear—abandonment. As a child, she lost her dad. My grandmother moved the four children to Ireland to live with my great granny because she couldn't raise four kids alone. Life there was primitive—thatched roof cottage, no running water, no electricity, seven people in three small rooms. Imagine the trauma of that move for a five-year-old girl. I believe it was life changing, actually scarring for her. Then after I was born, she lost her mom after a grueling battle with cancer. These painful losses were part of the can of worms she spoke of, yet refused to open. That can was toxic to her, to all of us really, for she refused to deal with the issues of the past that were driving her anxiety and explosive rages. It was more than menopause and an empty nest. I believe she had deep psychological pains that she buried. She carried this can for years and I believed she would never open it. She was simply too afraid.

To be clear, when I say mental illness, please know that it is not just what you see in movies, with people suffering from schizophrenia or psychotic episodes. Mental illness is so much more common and shows itself on a very wide scale. I believe it affects us all at some point, just like the flu. It is depression, anxiety, personality disorders, and more. It is the child with stomach pains afraid to go to school for months. It is the adult who struggles with a body image disorder. It is the parent or spouse whose personality is difficult, unpredictable, and distant. For most of us, our mental/emotional issues are not so severe that we can't live independent lives. Yet when left unchecked, any mental issue can limit our ability to live life in the most fulfilling ways we can. We need to remove the stigma of mental health and treat it as we do any other medical issue.

Looking back, I think my mom suffered from more than depression or anxiety. A lot of her behavior is consistent with Borderline Personality Disorder, where one experiences a palpable fear of abandonment, moments of severe paranoia, mood swings, and unstable relationships. I am not a doctor, just a child trying to make sense of the breakdown that stole my mom. It pains me so much to know that her life could have been so different had she only asked for help. I loved her. I wanted her in my life. But I needed the relationship to be healthy. So, I drew a line in the sand. I could not go down with the ship. I had to save myself if she wouldn't let me save the both of us.

That year was the toughest year of my life. I worked part time and lived on $40 a week (not much for clothes, food, and gas). I finished my last year of nursing school and graduated with honors while paying my own way. It was a lonely, difficult time with many sleepless, tear-filled nights. But I did it. I am a stronger woman because of it, having learned the true meaning of self-reliance. I lived alone for two years, and I was blessed to have a wonderful boyfriend—now husband of 25 years—love me. Ken taught me, for the first time in my life, the true power of unconditional love. It is as beautiful as it sounds, and I do deserve it.

We all do!

For many years, I blamed myself for the rift with my parents; I felt like the black sheep of the family. Heck, even my initials are BAA! I was rarely included in family events. Mom's fragility guided family interactions and since my presence made her uncomfortable, I was left out. For years I thought that if I had only played the game the way she wanted me to, maybe, just maybe, we would still be a "normal" family. But there was nothing normal about living with my mother's untreated mental illness. I know first hand that if left unchecked, it will destroy you and the people you love. We have to face it and work through it. That is why I share my story, her story; our story.

In the initial year after I moved out, Mom refused to speak to me, despite my continued outreach via cards and letters. I never saw another birthday card or Christmas gift. She refused to come to my wedding and wanted no part of my growing family. My dad did walk me down the aisle but did not reach out after that. He didn't have the nerve to stand up to her. Sadly, my parents never got to know my three sons, sit at one of their soccer games, or see them graduate. Life went on as if I had no parents at all. I was blessed with in-laws who filled the void as best as anyone could.

My dad passed away in 2000. We had a beautiful moment of reconciliation the day before he died; a real blessing for us both. He told me he loved me and was sorry for shutting me out. I have been told that I am a very forgiving person because throughout it all I didn't harbor any anger at my dad or anyone really. Maybe I should have. Dad did not stand by me. He let me walk away. He didn't fight for me. To this day I believed it slowly killed him—the regret and the sadness. I once ran into him while shopping with my 18-month-old son on my hip. I could see in his eyes how much it hurt to not know his grandson. But the power of our flawed family dynamics was too much for him. I chose to give him a pass; I knew what he was up against.

I did not expect other family members to deal with my mom as I did. I wish they would have confronted her as I had. Together, maybe we could have pushed her to get help. But I believe that each of us must handle pain and dysfunction on our own terms. I like to think that my family members did what they were capable of doing given the complexity of it all. They were caught up in a web of dysfunction. Guilt trips. Obligatory visits. Fear that mom would shut them out, too. Maybe I let them off easy. I'm okay with that. If I held on to anger, bitterness, and resentment, it would only have eaten me alive as well. I truly feel that forgiveness saved me. It is not about blindly accepting the hurt cast upon us but about making a conscious choice to not let it destroy us.

We all had hoped things would improve with Mom after Dad's death. They didn't. She kept me at bay. I eventually stopped sending cards, trying to reconcile. We had no relationship at all, living 15 minutes apart. We did progress to a point of being together at family gatherings; it was awkward but civil.

Our 27-year estrangement ended a few weeks before my 48th birthday. My mom passed away suddenly although peacefully with my siblings and I by her side. When a case of pneumonia took a turn for the worst, I knew I needed to stand by my family and say my goodbyes. I want to believe that she heard me when I told her that I loved her and was sorry for the lost time. I meant it wholeheartedly. I vowed that I would make sure my siblings and I would always have each other's back. What parent doesn't want that?

In the months since she passed, I have found the strength and the peace to finish this book. I began it four years ago, but at that time it had no resolution, no end. I was still in too much pain.

Now the wounds are beginning to heal. Oddly, it started with the experience of renovating her house before selling it. The house had fallen into disrepair as mom's health deteriorated over the years. It was as if they were symbiotic. My siblings and I rolled up our sleeves, like my parents did in days past, and we worked to bring light and love back into our childhood home. Who knew the joy that would come from ripping 1980s paneling off the wall? It was so cathartic!

I reconnected with an old friend of my mom. She told me that when I was four or five years old, she and my mom had talked about opening a decorating business together. Imagine—*Connie and Betty's Home Repair and Decorating Service.* That blew me away. Some 40 years later, I am bringing that business to life. I had no idea.

It has been a bittersweet journey cleaning out the house, finding all sorts of treasures and emotional triggers, too. The most profound moment was finding a box in the top of her closet. It held all the cards, photos and letters I had sent over the years, each one opened. Also in that box were cards and letters she wrote to me and never sent. Her words were calm and loving. She just never sent them! These cards delivered the healing words I needed from her.

I now fully understand that her mental illness was just stronger than her love for me.

This is hard to swallow. BUT that's just how powerful fear, anxiety, and depression are. They can drive you away from those you love most. The clarity this brings is life changing.

Knowing that I was loved regardless of her ability to show it was the piece that brings it all full circle.

Knowing that my worth is not measured by another's inability to appreciate me? Priceless.

Like I promised my mom, we kids stuck together and worked on renovating the house. It has been sold to a sweet young couple and is ready for a new story to be written there. The house was repaired while I began to heal myself with her tools in my hands. Hence the back cover photo—me in my childhood bedroom with her hammer in hand. So, while I couldn't fix my mom back then, I could fix her home now. And I know in my heart that she is proud of me!

Moving Past the Past

It's time to talk about the can again. Not the potty, but that can of worms you need to open. It's filled with the stuff you need to deal with so you can Flush the Fear and move on in life. Please open it for your partner, for your kids, and most importantly, OPEN IT for you!

My mom had so many great qualities, but she was afraid to deal with her stuff. This single flaw kept her from being all she could have been, and it truly tore our family apart. I watched this creative, smart, and capable woman driven into poor emotional and mental health by fear and anxiety and pride. She could have been a force to reckon with if she had only worked on herself with as much passion as she did on our house. She lived with a deep sense of fear and insecurity that I never saw until that storm hit. Hindsight is 20/20.

In my heart, I know our shifting roles in one another's lives was a key reason for the insanity we shared in 1991. I get that now, as a mom myself. I believe her hormonal shift and underlying emotional issues just made her incapable of coping with her emotions at the time. It was just too much all at once. She had invested so much of herself in her role as a mom; she was at a loss for her next role.

Being an involved parent is a wonderful gift to your family, but losing yourself in the process can be so destructive. As moms, we owe it to ourselves to never lose "us" under diapers, carpools, and the pile of dinner dishes. I truly believe if my mom had invested more into a job, friends, and her relationship with my dad, she could have weathered the storm better. She could have seen my growing up and growing away as a moment of pride and joy not something to be feared and halted.

She relied on her role in others' lives to give herself purpose and value. I think so many women of her time did. But I now understand that I was not responsible for her happiness. It was not my job to make her feel whole or give her purpose. Each of us must find that on our own. No parent should put that upon their child.

Fortunately, I am blessed that my siblings and I are still close. I believe they understand that I didn't abandon my parents. I saved myself. I wish I had understood that at the time, so I did not feel so responsible for all that happened and carry this sense of rejection for so long. I took all the blame deep in my soul. A piece of it still resides there, but it's getting smaller over time.

I have also learned that trying to understand another's perspective and what motivates them allows room for forgiveness. Being able to step back and see that 99% of the time, when someone hurts us, it is coming from their own issues—insecurity, fear of rejection, being alone, or losing control. It could be many things. It often has little to do with YOU. Fully embracing this idea helps you let it go. It lets you forgive. Forgiveness equals healing. It is then that you can stop defining your worth by what expectations others have for you.

It has taken me almost three decades to grasp this. I have moments when I am still a scared, lonely, young woman begging for acceptance and unconditional love. I have accepted that my parents did the best they knew how with the experiences they had to learn from, and that they loved me the way they knew how. I find peace in knowing that someday when we meet in the afterlife, that unconditional love will know no boundaries. For now, I work hard to be the kind of parent to my own children that I know my mother could have been had she only invested more into herself.

Everything I went through was life changing. In retrospect, I see it all as a gift. I had the opportunity to face my most difficult life challenge at a young age and I came out on the other side stronger and healthier. I make a conscious choice every day to not dwell on the negative, to not blame anyone for the circumstances. It is what it is. I do have a duty to help others avoid the mistakes that were made and not only survive a tough relationship but thrive despite it.

There were many days on my own when I felt defeated, unloved, and broken. I could have turned to drugs or alcohol to cope. I could have become self-destructive, absorbed by the anger and pain. We can wear our pain like a badge, or we can forgive. We can be a victim or a hero. It is a choice. Do we let bad things define us or are we going to put behind us? I say, "Let it go."

It's Time For A Movement

As we identify the root of our fears, we are more empowered to move past them because we can't fight the unknown. Now is as good a time as any for you to get moving. Admit it, the thought of holding on to your negative crap for even one more day just stinks! It means more angst and more pain and less of YOU being happy. It doesn't have to be this way.

I want you to join me in a movement, a movement that is cleansing and powerful. No kale smoothies involved; I promise. This is an emotional cleansing. One that involves one simple idea: Letting Go.

Letting It Go

Let It Go. Let It Go!!! If you have young daughters, you may be envisioning a sparkly Elsa from *Frozen* on an icy mountain top breaking out in song. It's a powerful movie scene. But seriously, letting go of fear and negativity is an incredibly powerful and courageous act. It is life changing.

We don't need grand Disney imagery to remind us that we all face fear; little fears and some big, scary ones, too. Small fears and anxieties are everywhere, like missing the morning train or getting a work assignment done on time. These things make us unsettled and nervous for the moment. Sometimes we are faced with big fears, the life altering kind — worrying about your partner relapsing into addiction or waiting for the results of your latest breast biopsy.

From medical concerns to worries about gun violence or global warming, fear rises when we can't necessarily stop things from happening. Fear of the unknown is a commonly used definition of anxiety. Every day, we face situations where we cannot control the outcome, but we can control our reaction to them.

Teaching Our Kids to Live Fearlessly

What if we lived in a world not driven by fear? We would be calmer, happier people. It would be a gift for ourselves and for our children. The future welfare of society depends on us teaching our children how to live in a world driven by positivity, not fear. We can't control the media and other outside forces but we can teach our kids (and ourselves) how to keep our worries in perspective so they don't cripple us.

As a parent, I have seen far too many moms and dads raising fear-focused kids. I was one of them! I grew up with a mom who worried about everything, so I learned to worry and obsess. I worried until I had stomach aches, Irritable Bowel Syndrome, and panic attacks as a young woman. I lived with my stomach in knots until the day my doctor offered me Xanax. I was 20 years old. I said, "No way." I was not going down that route. I turned instead to running and a therapist. While I am much better today at letting go of my crap, I still must work hard to not project my own fears and anxieties onto my boys. It is hard to keep fear at bay when all we want is to do is protect our kids. Protecting them doesn't mean paralyzing them with our own angst. What we need to do is to arm our kids with skills to manage life's challenges on their own!

We all know the parents who haven't cut the cord yet. They are so busy flying the helicopter; obsessing about red dye #5, bubble wrapping the kids and passing out trophies to everyone. I know that sounds harsh. Please know I'm not trying to shame anyone, but mental health experts will confirm, this is hurting our kids' personal development and sense of autonomy. Yes, of course, there is an age-appropriate time to let kids do for themselves. There is also a time to let them go! If you are piloting your kids' every move, you need to stop. It is hard to turn off the parental protection instinct, but it is time to put down the controls and teach them to fly solo. We can change the narrative for our kids.

Today, the rate of mental health issues in our young adults is skyrocketing. More teens are medicated for depression and anxiety than ever before and we are all in serious danger if we continue to raise a generation of young people who live in fear and angst. It is so crippling, and you can see its impact in the rise of addiction and suicide. Kids are faced with more stress than we were and they are struggling to cope with failure, disappointment, and lack of belonging. We need to give them the tools to cope when these tough things happen, because they will. We need to let them get dirty, scrape a knee, and learn from failing. We need to say "No" sometimes. It's okay for them to be disappointed. We need to *let them experience things that make them feel uncomfortable while we are near to guide them through it instead of creating an environment that lets them avoid it.*

Let them learn for themselves how to make choices, age appropriately of course. Give your kids the tools to guard themselves against the "dangers" out there, teaching them to think for themselves. You can't be their invisible shield forever. They need to know what to do when you aren't there. When I was 12 years old, a girl in school told me that I was fat. I cried so much. What my dad said to comfort me then has never left me: "Don't let anyone screw up your day, they're just not worth it!" Wise words.

Teach your kids to manage life's negativity now and they will rise to the occasion and live with a positive mindset later! There is a great book on this called *Blessings of a Skinned Knee* by Wendy Mogel, PhD. It is based on Jewish principles of growth through failures—a powerful read for parents of any faith.

Our children will teach us a life lesson or two if we stop to listen. I remember a time when my oldest son was five and he went to a pool party. On the ride home, I asked him what he did at the party. He said he watched the other kids play water tag. Well, my heart broke. I envisioned my mild-mannered son sitting by himself, distanced from the group, watching others have fun. What mean kids they were not to include him, I thought. Did the parents see him alone? Did they ignore him? I asked him why he didn't play tag.

This little old soul responded, "Mommy, I just don't like water tag. That's how God made me."

I began to cry. My five-year-old was completely comfortable in his own skin. He wasn't insecure or uncomfortable on the sideline. He knew what he liked and what he didn't like. He was okay with watching. Who the hell am I to push on him my own insecurities and childhood hurts of being left out? He gave me the best parenting lesson ever—to not cast my fears upon him. He is now 22 and the most well-adjusted secure young man I have ever met. He doesn't remember the party or the conversation, but I will never forget it.

I know you don't want to saddle your kids with the same kind of neurosis your parents bestowed on you. Frankly, no one wants that kind of inheritance. The next generation will surely pack their own emotional baggage over time. What we can do is lighten their load by showing them how we can move out of the state of Fear and into the state of Living. Lead by example.

A few years ago, on a vacation in Mexico, I had a bold moment and decided to cliff jump. It was a roped-off area along a river designated for jumps, so it was safe and regulated. I climbed up there enthusiastically and then I panicked. It was high, 17 feet high! I peered over the edge several times and walked away. I was about to climb back down the ladder when I saw my boys in the water floating on their tubes cheering me on. What lesson would I teach them if I climbed down? They would see fear instead of courage driving my next move. I took a breath, held my nose and ran off the cliff. AND it was freaking awesome!

I know the mental transition from the dark to the light can be tough. Like I said, I was raised in an anxious environment of whatever can go wrong, will go wrong. Mom was always waiting for the other shoe to drop. It has taken me years to move past that mentality. I know fear has many of you stuck, too. You are afraid to break out of that trap. It is all you know; your modus operandi. Stepping outside the comfort zone may seem scarier than the negative world you are used to, but I truly believe that LIFE begins when you get *uncomfortable*, when you challenge the status quo. When you say "NO" to fear, and "YES" to life! This was true for me. Join me in moving away from fear. It can be life changing and it starts with sharing.

Share a Square

You Seinfeld fans surely remember that iconic scene with Elaine Benes stuck in a stall, desperate for a square of TP. She begged the gal in the adjacent stall to simply *spare a square*, to give up one measly little piece of paper so she could wipe her backside, because dirty bums stink. All Elaine wanted was to come clean. Hey, don't you want to do that, too?

You should want to come clean; with yourself and with others in your life. It leads to Flushing the Fear. When it comes to coming clean, I count on two-ply paper to get the job done! Yeah, I'm talking about two-ply toilet paper. It is a tool for an emotional exercise I call **Share a Square**.

During live Flush the Fear presentations, I throw rolls of toilet paper into the audience. Yep, I feel like Oprah tossing the keys to new cars at people, saying "You get a roll, you get a roll." Everybody gets a roll, well, at least a square. I ask them to *Share a Square* and pass the roll to the person beside them.

After the TP is adequately distributed, I ask my audience to dig deep, deep into their own soul, and be honest with themselves. I want them to come clean and identify that one big fear, or that one negative or self-deprecating thought that is holding them back in life. I challenge them to literally write it down on a square of toilet paper. Seeing and confronting the fear makes it real, gives it shape and lets you separate from it. A 2012 article from Harvard Health points out the benefit of creating a worry box: whenever angst arises, you write your concerns on slips of paper and deposit them in a shoebox. Writing it out is incredibly powerful, cathartic and… can I say, a moving experience.

In my presentations, I next invite the crowd to join me at the edge of the stage, where they can bravely and ceremoniously *Flush the Fear.* In a moment of courage, they drop their square in my toilet and Let It Go.

In case you are wondering, it is a real toilet that I bring to the stage. Bold, odd, crazy! Yes, all of the above. But you know what is even crazier? After a mere 45-minute talk, people are ready and willing to share with such raw honesty that it completely blows me away. I feel honored that men, women, and teens are willing to be so vulnerable, so open in that safe, quiet moment I created for them.

Many of the squares have brought me to tears — the pain, the anxiety, and the insecurities they speak of is so real, so powerful. It is truly a moving experience for me and I believe it is for them as well.

These squares are shared with me anonymously. The identity of each flusher is unknown. I have no idea who has shared what fear, nor do I want to. My toilet is simply a vessel to help them *let it go*, even for just a moment. Throughout the book, I will share images of the squares that have been flushed away in my Potty Talk. The squares I share in this book are generic in nature and can't be linked to any one person. A ghost writer has rewritten them in different handwriting to protect the privacy of each author.

It is with great respect that I share their words with you, because their fears are your fears and my fears, too. My goal is to remind you that you are not alone. There is great comfort in knowing others have walked in your shoes. Healing begins when we feel understood, safe, and supported. Awesomeness begins when we let go of the crap.

Part Two: Tools For Living

What got me through the most traumatic time in my life? I have come to understand that I was packing one hell of a toolbox at 21 years old. And by tools, I mean life skills, attitude, chutzpah. At the time, I felt like I was just getting by, but now I see I had the right stuff to survive. Maybe some of these skills are innate; optimism and faith played a part, too. I didn't just use these tools then; I have been using them everyday since. I believe we can all learn to use the tools I am about to share for our own self-improvement.

The "tools" in my toolbox carry very valuable lessons about self-reliance, thriving, and living fearlessly. They are symbols of the stuff we need to get through this journey called life, especially motherhood. There is a lot to work through—from career and family to our own emotional baggage. You need the right tools so you can not only DO IT YOURSELF, but do it *for* yourself.

Because the greatest DIY project you will ever tackle is YOU!

Hands-On Homework

As we open this toolbox, remember that every DIYer needs a workroom—a place to get down and dirty. I have created space for you to do your work, where you can take notes and be honest with yourself. I'll be asking you to Share a Square later. I want you to write your fears on some TP and let it go!

We'll focus on improving the roles most of us play in life; partner, parent, employee, child, and friend. But we cannot forget about the most important role we each play...being ourselves! I want you to use this book as a guide as you read and think about how you can improve your life. Write in it, highlight stuff, whatever moves you! As you fill in the blanks, go with your gut instinct. It is usually spot on. Trust it. Grab a pen and some wine if you like, and get ready to identify what is holding you back from being a better YOU. Let's open our metaphorical toolbox and Flush the Fear.

IT'S HAMMER TIME

Emily Dickinson once said, "It is better to be the hammer than the anvil."

It's a powerful and beautiful quote. It struck me in two ways. The first is this: just as the hammer drives a nail into wood to make a lasting bond, YOU are the driving force behind building your relationships.

You've gotta be a hammer in your own life creating strong lasting bonds with other people. These bonds are critical to our well-being and our mental health. Being connected to others gives us the courage to stand up to our fears! The hammer crushes the fear of going it alone.

A key psychological theory by Abraham Maslow describes a hierarchy of needs and points to our desire for belonging and love. It is the third need in the pyramidal image he created to explain human motivators. He believed that we must meet certain needs and once we secure them, we can move upward to the next level. Sometimes we move between the levels at different stages of life. He said we have five levels of need: 1) basics of life — food and water; 2) shelter and security; 3) love and belonging; 4) esteem and recognition; and lastly 5) self-actualization. He describes that last level as self-awareness and a readiness to fulfill one's potential.

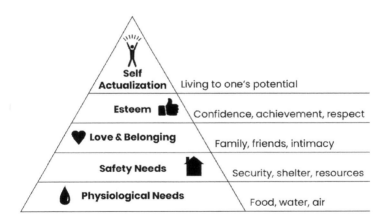

It may seem deep at first, but I think it is brilliant and quite simple to understand. The desire and need for love and belonging comes into play after we are fed and safe. Our friendships, romantic partnerships, and families fill this core need. We use our social, community, or religious groups to give our human connections a deeper purpose. Barbara Streisand sang it well: "People, people who need people are the luckiest people in the world!" Call me a dork but I am a total Babs fan and she hit the nail on the head with those lyrics! We really do need each other. No man is an island.

In today's world filled with so much automation, it is easy to lose touch with our humanity and with each other. We interact with our laptops and phones, and even talk to our cars on a regular basis. Texting and emojis have replaced the spoken word and the real emotions behind them. Of course, our modern technology tools are time savers, but they can be real relationship killers.

How do we fight the assault on our human relationships? Those shiny, sleek devices in our pockets are so tempting, so intriguing as we ignore the interesting, complex, unique humans sitting across the dinner table, or worse yet, the one sharing the bed with us.

I recently saw a family of four on vacation. Two little girls no older than three sat strapped into highchairs, each with an iPad watching cartoons over their breakfast. The parents were on their own phones. No one talked or interacted. What a lost moment. A meal is a great time to connect. They could have asked these girls about their favorite part of yesterday, what was exciting about the day ahead or how yummy the Fruit Loops were. But no. A beautiful moment was lost. Gone.

We need to preserve our relationships, to breathe life back into them before it's too late. We are more focused on our Wi-Fi connectivity than our human connections! It's time for CPR — Cell Phone Resistance. Can you do it? Can you put down the phone and turn off the computer? Are you willing to disconnect to reconnect? It's hard but we try it in our house. The dinner table is a phone-free zone. Being present is a priority.

The desire for connection is real and we try to use those phones for that. Why do you think social media thrives? We are addicted to the idea of connecting, relating, and getting affirmation. But you need real connections, not just Likes and Follows. There's no substitute for a core group of people who've got your back, who want to know you and accept you as you are. Connecting is the tool that gets you through life's challenges. It got me through mine.

When my life began to unravel, I initially didn't let anyone know what was happening at home. My family looked so together and "normal." I hid all my struggles until I started going down with the ship. Once I opened up to Dr. A, my friends, and my therapist, I found the strength to set the boundaries that I needed to preserve my own sanity and wellbeing. Most importantly, I realized I was not alone. Many people had tough family stuff like mine. I was able to have women my mom's age give me insight on how my mom felt watching her role in life change. This allowed me to find compassion and understanding for my mom's actions. Opening up to others gives you a perspective you can't have when you're stuck in your own head, replaying the same story over again.

I desperately wanted my mom to talk to someone about her issues. It could have been a game changer. Had she talked to other moms with empty nests and changing roles, she may have not felt so alone. She may have been able to better understand her feelings and know all parents go through this. She may not have vilified me for having a life outside of her and I wouldn't have this story to share!

The first time you tell others your painful story can be scary. You have to open that damn can of worms. How will he take the news you share? Will she judge you or shame you? Will they dismiss your feelings and fears? Let's be positive instead of fearful. What if they embrace you? What if they tell you they had a similar experience to share? Maybe letting the painful words roll off your lips is the first step in changing your life.

Going to therapy changed my life. It taught me perspective, compassion, and grace, not only for my mom, but for myself as well. It taught me not to assume, not to judge, and not to place myself in a position to be hurt again. It gave me the tools to survive the greatest challenge of my life. The power of connection made this possible. The power of sharing. The power of vulnerability.

For some of you, this requires baby steps because you haven't left your comfort zone in a while. Your walls are up. Maybe your own can is packed so tightly that you are terrified to open it. That's okay. Others have opened theirs and are able to guide you. Today is a new day. You can set a goal for today, tomorrow or this week. Challenge yourself to connect. Envision yourself as that hammer.

The hammer is a great tool. It is strong, but it is not a passive tool. It needs you to drive it. It needs you to do the work for it to connect the nail to the wood. You are the driving force. If you want a love life that is fulfilling, you gotta make your partner a priority so your passion and connection stays strong. Want to succeed in business? Get out to network and grow your circle of influence. Do you want to stop feeling alone and depressed? Put yourself out there. Want people to care, to help you? Let them know what you need. This idea of building strong relationships hinges on you getting out there, showing up, making an effort, and reaching out.

Family Connections — Building a Stronger Family

Do you feel disconnected from your kids? Do you feel a little empty watching them growing up too fast? OMG, YES. It's killing me. I understand how my mom felt when I was leaving the nest. Wasn't it just yesterday that my guys were wearing footie pajamas snuggled in my arms with a blankie and a binkie? As the years go on, you can't let the passing of time create a disconnection.

You know that old Cat Stevens song, "Cat's in the Cradle"? It has so much more meaning now as a parent listening to the story of a dad who never seemed to have time for his son and then regretted his son had grown to be just like him. The power of bonding with your kids was lost on this dad until it was too late.

What can you do to connect more deeply with your kids? If they are little, play with them! Sit on the floor. Build a puzzle. Cook with them. Ride bikes. Teach them to fix something! If they are older, trap them in a car for 30 minutes to talk. I get more candid conversations with my guys in a car than anywhere else. You have a captive audience, and it's easier for some to open up when they don't have to make eye contact. (It helps if you listen to their music on the way.) If they are adult kids, offer them a brunch outing. No one ever turns down a free breakfast! Create a space and time to strengthen that bond you share. Or start building one that is missing! Your kids will not forget those moments. When you get down on their level and connect with them, they see someone fun and approachable. They feel safe opening up to you. This feeling sets a great foundation for the teen years, when they think you are a big dork but like you enough to converse about their world and let you in.

This kind of connection with your kids alleviates fear for both of you. It lets you understand where their head is and it reminds them that you are there for them, unconditionally. Unfortunately, my mom was not. She had a completely different view of the world. Like I said before, hers was often colored by fear and angst. I couldn't share my feelings about a boyfriend or worries about school. I had to hold it together because I couldn't add more to her already full plate of worry.

Our kids need us to be there for them. They need us to have done the work we need to do so we can be parents who are healthy and have a comfortable grasp on life. It is really hard to help our kids navigate life when we have our hands so full of our own baggage that we can't hold theirs. I had to turn to other women in my life for support. It should have been my mom that I leaned on. I want your kids coming to you for that safe, open space to be heard, to be validated, and to be loved. Remember though, sometimes your child's concerns are far more complicated than those outlined in your Parenting 101 book. There is no shame in seeking help for yourself or your child. You don't have to do it alone. Having your ducks in a row helps you embrace the situation and together, you can find the professional help that your family needs.

Connecting on your kids' level doesn't have to be hard. I know their taste in music, TV, and means of communication is so far removed from our days of MTV and the princess phone, but if listening to some crappy rap music makes them think you're cool, suck it up. It lets you get closer to them and maybe get a glimpse of what they are thinking about and facing in life! Ask them questions: what do they know of modern politics? Why do they like this rapper? Who do they admire in their life? Listen to them without judgment. Hold your snarky response even if they say Post Malone is more talented than Prince. Of course, they are totally wrong, but keep it to yourself!

Not knowing what your kids are into and who they are becoming makes you an anxious parent. I get it. You fear the unknown influences on their life. Keep lines of communication open and there are fewer things for you to worry about. Communication and transparency keep a family whole.

Before I moved out, my mom's anxiety had reached such intensity that when I was getting home later than expected, I was accosted with yelling, not relief that I made it home. She had visions of me kidnapped or in a ditch! You may worry when you don't hear from your kids or they are late but don't let your fear paralyze the relationship. Be calm. Tell them you are so glad they are home safe. Tell them you were worried and that next time you need them to communicate, to connect and let you know their ETA. It's a simple, respectful request. It empowers them to step up and lets them know you are trusting their ability to be out on their own. Of course, coming home all hours of the night and being unaccounted for is another story, but dumping your crazy on them for being ten minutes late only drives them away. Trust me!

The open and transparent relationship is good for you both. It adds trust and bonding and reduces anxiety. Who wouldn't love to have a less stressful experience raising kids? My relationship with my kids has been vastly different than mine with my parents. I work hard every day to change that narrative, and you can, too.

The Love Connection

Don't forget to keep the fire burning with the love of your life. My husband and I have been together over 25 years and we joke that we still like each other. Not every moment has been wedded bliss. That only happens in fairy tales. We have our struggles. But we keep working at it. It takes a conscious effort to stay present and connected. Marriage is tough. Kids, jobs, parents, and volunteer gigs all get in the way. We must carve out those times when we put each other at the top of the list. Make date nights, get into bed early, and connect — and by connect, yes, I am talking about sex! There's no stronger way for two people to connect than on an intimate level of mutual love. Respect the power of the love that brought you together in the first place.

When you are truly connected to your partner, you find security and peace in your relationship. You know where you stand and having that security gives you the strength to deal whatever else life throws at you. Your partner has your back and you have theirs. Nothing is more powerful than that unconditional love and a sense of belonging.

You've Got a Friend

The power of connection is vital to the end and doesn't only come from children and romantic partners. It can come from meaningful friendships. A May 2014 *Huffington Post* article cited interviews a nurse had with dying patients. The nurse shared the top regrets of the dying. At the #4 spot: "I wish I had stayed in touch with my friends." Simple idea but it was a big regret.

Real friends make us laugh, call us on our shit, and always have our back! We shouldn't wait until our dying days to appreciate them. My husband tells me he is a bit envious of my large circle of friends. I did not have that as a kid. Believe it or not, I was quite quiet and shy. With age, I grew bolder and more outgoing, but I also put in the time investing in my friendships. When you do, they are there for you when the poo hits the fan! Not sure how to open up to new friends? Try these easy techniques.

Host a party. Surely you have a friend, relative, neighbor, or acquaintance who sells skincare or cookware. Invite a few people over for a demo, and encourage them to bring others. You draw people into your world, but you don't have to be the center of attention. You might even get new pots and pans out of the deal! Why not join a book club? You get to hear others share their thoughts and insights and share yours without the conversation being about you. The book binds you with a shared experience. Look for activities that you can share with others. It is a subtle way to find your place in a group without approaching a total stranger saying, "Hi, can we be friends?"

After a while, you may feel confident enough to plan that girls' night out or have the neighbors in for cocktails like our parents did in the disco age. No matter how you do it, be sure to make time for friends, even if it's "just catching up" phone calls. You want to make sure you have people at your funeral, right? Just kidding, but you get the point. Friends make life bearable. And that leads to…

Winnie the Pooh. He was a wise old bear. He once said, "You can't stay in your corner of the Forest waiting for others to come to you. You have to go to them sometimes." He's right, you know. No one is going to make connections for you. You've gotta Do It Yourself.

I spent a lot of time on connection because it is the most important tool of all. Another famed psychologist, Erik Erikson, listed connection and intimacy as a key stage to healthy human growth and development. Without it, we can be stuck in a state of isolation and depression. VeryWell Mind (2019) states, "Erikson believed that having a fully formed sense of self (established during the identity versus confusion stage) is essential to being able to form intimate relationships. People with a poor sense of self tend to have less committed relationships and are more likely to suffer emotional isolation, loneliness, and depression."

He points out that that intimacy doesn't have to be of a romantic nature. Friends, family, roommates, and coworkers can successfully make up the tribe of people who love you and "get" you. Let's not forget that connecting with yourself more deeply can help you better connect with others. So sometimes you need to plan a day to reconnect with YOU.

So many of the TP confessions I get are about a lack of connection. People worried about losing loved ones, not having friends, and being left out. The isolation we all experienced during the Coronavirus pandemic was so challenging because we simply need each other, especially in hard times. It was crippling at times for so many. Our deep connections with people genuinely make life worth living. That is why support groups and social clubs are so successful. We want to find people with shared experiences and goals. We attach ourselves to others because we want to belong. We were never meant to go it alone. The power of connection will let us thrive, not just survive everything else this crazy world dishes up!

Don't let the fear of being alone hold you down.

Alone. It is a scary concept. Humans are innately social creatures so we fear being abandoned, left out, and disconnected. With a hammer in your hand, you can connect more deeply with the people who have your back, your hand, and your heart.

Put yourself out there. Be a hammer. Connect.

It's time to Do It Yourself. What can you do today, this week, or this month to connect with others?

As a parent _____

As a partner _____

As a child _____

As a friend _____

In business _____

THE ACME ANVIL

"It is better to be the hammer than the anvil." - Emily Dickinson

If you were lucky enough to grow up in the 1970s or 80s, you probably remember Looney Tunes, where Wile E. Coyote drops an Acme-brand anvil on his nemesis Road Runner, or at least he tries. As a kid, I thought it was mindless entertainment. As a parent, I think OMG, we watched this? These two were out for blood, and dropping an anvil on someone's head

would certainly inflict pain! In the cartoon world, such an assault leaves no lasting scars. That's not true in real life, is it?

While many of you only know the anvil from the coyote's pranks, its true purpose relates back to the work of a blacksmith or ironworker. The anvil's job is to sit quietly and still on the workbench and take a beating. That is a crappy job. The blacksmith's hammer pounds on it again and again and again as the hot metal is reshaped. The molten metal sustains blow after blow until it bears no resemblance to its original state. In the process, the anvil too is scarred.

Do you ever feel like an anvil, beaten down by life? Maybe you feel like a doormat for others? I believe Emily Dickinson was right — it *is* far better to be the hammer. No one relishes the idea of being beaten down, scarred. Yet we allow it to happen in little ways every day and sometimes in really big ways, too. The anvil is a tool to remind us of the dangers of unhealthy relationships.

I suppose we have all been an anvil for someone at some point. We have been on the receiving end of someone's blow. Now, I digress to say that I hope to God that if you are reading this and are in an abusive situation, you tell someone you trust and find a way out. No one deserves to be physically or emotionally abused — NOT EVER. It is not your fault. You do not deserve it. Please confide in someone; email me if you don't know where to turn. I am serious about that. My email is on my website listed on the back of the book. We'll find you help. It goes back to Maslow's hierarchy of needs — you deserve safety and security.

Most of us are not exposed to an abusive anvil-like situation, but we still encounter those moments when we feel like the mole in Whack-a-Mole! You might feel like you just got whacked upside the head by a spouse's snarky comment, a demeaning boss, or an ungrateful child. Maybe your spouse belittles your contribution to the family, your mother-in-law drops a snide hint about some weight gain, or a friend just imposes her kids on you for the afternoon, AGAIN! People take advantage of us, knock us down or make us the scapegoat for their issues. It happens. I am guilty of being a doormat. I have put out the "You're WELCOME to use me" mat on many occasions. You know, that doormat that says you are invited to hurt me, not value my time or talents, and let me feel responsible because your life is unhappy. We all have experienced this at some point.

Toxic relationships are poisonous to our heart and minds. They leave us questioning our worth and our sanity. It's easy to be taken in by people who are more wily than Wile E. Coyote himself, engaging you sweetly while secretly planning to drop an anvil on your head. You know those people, the ones who befriend you, take advantage of your kindness, and stab you in the back. Ouch. That hurts.

It is often hard to identify those coyotes in disguise. I have come to find that these folks are usually dealing with psychological disorders, often narcissism, plain and simple. They are people in our families, in our office, and even in our bed.

Per Psychology Today, by definition, a narcissist has the following behaviors:

- A grandiose sense of self-importance
- Preoccupation with fantasies of unlimited success, power, brilliance, beauty, or ideal love
- Belief that one is special and can only be understood by or associate with special people or institutions
- A need for excessive admiration
- A sense of entitlement (to special treatment)
- Exploitation of others
- A lack of empathy
- Envy of others or the belief that one is the object of envy
- Arrogant, haughty behavior or attitudes

People with personality disorders exhibit particular types of behavior that manifest in often destructive ways. I share this info because I think it is important to understand if you are in a toxic relationship. I really wish someone had clued me in years before I broke away from my mother. Consider yourself warned. Many people will label such a personality as mean or simply a "bitch." There are psychological diagnoses for such disorders; Narcissistic, Borderline, Antisocial Personality and more. The traits of these disorders can be overwhelming for those who have them, as well as for everyone around them. Those with these disorders are masters of manipulation and have a pattern of blaming others for their own shortcomings. They suck us into their drama until we are hurting, too. They often leave us thinking that we are the crazy one!

I shared this excerpt from Psychology Today because it so clearly lays out this type of character that we have all encountered. Remember there is a sliding scale for this behavior. Some people are mild, while others are outrageously manipulative. It was not until I was an adult that I started to piece together my mom's behavior. She clearly had some borderline and narcissistic tendencies as well as other issues. At the time, I saw it as unreasonable, hurtful, and out of control.

I don't believe these folks mean to be destructive. I think they are genuinely unhappy people who take it out on the rest of us because they haven't dealt with their shit. They often don't understand the depth of the damage they inflict on others. Some do and just don't care. Most are just incapable of the empathy needed to stop the cycle. Sound like anyone you know?

Overall, they are very clever, calculating people who arrive in your life full of warmth and energy and draw you in until you're under their sway, then they show you their true colors! Watch out for these people. Their energy is so hot, so blazing that it will burn you, like the metal in the iron shop. But no worries; get burned once and you'll be better at seeing past their smoke and mirrors the next time one rolls into your life.

Being a doormat with family and friends is an easy situation to get into. We don't want to say "no" to people we care about. That would be wrong, right? Not really. We often let people walk all over us, narcissists or not. Siblings, parents, friends, and even our own kids. I must digress a moment to focus on the kids. In recent years, I have seen so many kids who are out of control, over-indulged, and given few limits. They rule the roost and boss their parents around. I never would have gotten away with that.

If we got "the look" from Mom, we fell into line. Even though there was never any serious consequence to the look, it was scary enough to make us behave!

There have been many times that I have had to bite my tongue with my kid's friends. Sometimes I just can't. I remember my son's friend yelling at his mom in my kitchen. I just could not just stand there silent. If she wasn't going to put him in his place, I was. She deserved respect, even if she wouldn't ask for it. Yes, it was ballsy. I politely told him that he was not to speak to his mother or any other adult that way, especially in my home. I *suggested* he apologize to her and make his request again with respect. He looked at me funny, but he did it. He has since told my son that I'm scary. LOL. I am cool with that! Maybe he will think twice about his manners in the future.

Teaching our kids simple kindness and respect from a young age will keep those narcissistic tendencies to a minimum. I shake my head when I see brats mouthing off to their parents, but I remind myself that these parents are allowing them to do it. People, including children, will mistreat us as often as we lay on the doorstep and say, "tread on me!"

We can't *allow* others to control our decisions, wants, and needs. I specifically used the word "allow." Narcissists, Borderlines, and the like only have the upper hand if we let them. It's time to call them on their BS and say "no" to being manipulated. I know you may be thinking, "This is easy for you to say, you don't know my situation... no one knows how unrealistic my dad is... you don't know what my wife is like." Yes, I may not know your specific story, but I lived it. At 21, I made a conscious choice to say "NO" to manipulation, resentment, and guilt. I stood up for what was healthy for me and what I needed to do for myself. I will never regret that nor apologize for it. Neither should you.

I remember the time after I moved out when I asked my mom to stop yelling at me over the phone. It was so upsetting, and she could be so relentless. I said I couldn't get on the phone if she was going to berate me. She hung up! That call would be the last time she ever picked up the phone to call me. It hurt that she chose anger over me, but I learned to accept it. Preserving my sanity was my priority. Please know that I am in no way encouraging you to say "To hell with my family. I'll do what I want to do." That is not the point. What I'm encouraging is self-respect and healthy boundaries.

I did not walk away without a fight to keep our family together. I went into therapy and learned how to set limits on the behaviors that were destructive. When you stop allowing others to treat you poorly, you must be prepared for some backlash. I got plenty. My mom was not prepared for me to stand up for myself. I had never been one to talk back or go against the grain. I walked on eggshells, not knowing what her next reaction would be. That is no way to live and one of the reasons why I left. Setting up boundaries is vital. We need an invisible dome that narcissism, criticism, and controlling behavior cannot penetrate. We cannot allow others to make unrealistic, unhealthy demands of our time and energy.

YOU are not to be an anvil to anyone. Not your parents, your partner, your kids, or your boss. Don't allow others to pound away at your potential and your dreams. Let's stop letting others smash your sense of self. You deserve respect, kindness, and unconditional love. Accept nothing less.

It begins with you loving yourself unconditionally. Start now. One small act of kindness towards yourself is saying, "I respect me!"

Say goodbye to being a doormat.

Standing up for yourself is one of the toughest things to do, especially when you have been conditioned to be passive and unappreciated. That has to end today. You deserve better.

It's time to Do It Yourself. What can you do today, this week, or this month to show yourself respect and have others treat you well?

I will respect myself...

As a parent by_____

As a partner by_____

As a child by_____

As a friend by_____

In business by_____

6

I GOTTA LEVEL WITH YOU

This self-improvement stuff is hard work, but this next tool is an easy one to use — a standard level with an air bubble in a water chamber. Maybe you have used it to hang a shelf or straighten a picture. It is a simple tool about balance. You angle it up or down until that little bubble is perfectly centered. Umm, bring the left up, now down just a smidge. There. Don't move! It's perfect.

Balance is not easy to maintain. Many of us try to keep life in perfect balance and I say try because it is nearly impossible to do. Personally, I think this notion of life balance is bullshit. And it is making us unhappy. The level helps us let go of the fear of being imperfect and the stress of doing it all!

The pursuit of perfection is making us nuts! We are sick and tired and stressed. Many of us walk around feeling overwhelmed by life. We wear so many hats, but we have only one head. We try to be perfect in all our roles all the time. We exhaust ourselves in the process. WHY do we do this? Because others think we should? Because the media tells us we can bring home the bacon, fry it up in a pan and never let him forget he's a man? I loved that Enjoli commercial as a kid, but now I think, *are you kidding? Who wants to live up to that?*

This level reminds me to level with myself. My life doesn't have to be in perfect balance. It may require some tough choices. Shit happens. That's okay. We're only human!

We juggle jobs, kids, partners, aging parents, friends, community, and sometimes, just sometimes, we toss ourselves in there. HOLY crap that is a lot of balls to juggle! Even the best jugglers drop one every now and then. Do you boo the juggler because he dropped one ball, or do you cheer him on because he kept six others in the air? You applaud, of course. So, I ask you, when do we cut ourselves a break as life falls out of whack? Some days as a mom with little ones under foot, just getting a shower a huge accomplishment. Celebrate the wins, not the misses.

The Mommy Mode

I think moms are the least forgiving people on the planet; forgiving of themselves, that is. We think we have to do everything and do it perfectly. We create more stress for ourselves by upholding ridiculously high standards. You know those cupcakes for the class party? Oh no, we can't buy them from the grocery store. Maybe a high-end bakery is acceptable but what will the other mommies think if they are not homemade and iced in the properly coordinated school colors? So, we drive out of the way to go to the store for food coloring, letting out a sigh as we pass the aisle of premade baked goods and stay up until midnight baking the darn things.

Who are you doing this for? Your kid, the other moms? It's certainly not for you. This is just the kind of the nonsense that we put ourselves through. This is the crap we buy into. Have I done it? Oh yeah. But I stopped and you can, too.

We should feel okay knowing that our time and money can only afford "X." I only started getting this into my own head a few years ago. It is so freeing. Be selective about where you spend your energy, your hours, and your Abe Lincolns. If the task involves something that is meaningful and important to the kids, then by all means do it. If you are baking those cupcakes with the kids, great! If not, just buy the grocery store treats and call it a day. They will remember the *time you spend with them* more than the *money you spend on them*. You may want to read that last sentence again! Balance is about choices.

House Beautiful

Another hat we don is part of the maid uniform. What if a neighbor stops by and our house looks "lived in"? Disgraceful isn't it? You mean your home doesn't always look like a Pinterest post? Mine does... NOT. When I had my first kid, it was pretty close. Honestly it was ridiculous; my house was immaculate. I wore that like a badge of honor, I admit it. But with each son I had, the house got a bit dirtier and more out of control. So what? My house is neat, fairly organized but far from immaculate. Growing up, you could eat off my mom's kitchen floor. I am not so sure this was a good thing. I wish she let that go and spent time being with us instead of cleaning! Consider what you want your legacy to be. My tombstone won't say, "Beloved homemaker." It will say, "Kick-ass mom and wife," because that's what matters. Stop thinking you need to keep the perfect house. Safe and livable and welcoming is good enough.

Truth is, if you keep a spotless house, you stress out the rest of us, because we feel the need to keep up! We all have dust bunnies; embrace them and think of them as furry pets without vet bills!

I teased a girlfriend once because she told me she cleans her house at 10 or 11 p.m. because she can't get it done during the day. (She was a stay-at-home mom like me, so I figured she has some time during the day.) I asked her when she makes time for sex. She laughed. She and her hubby weren't making time for that. A week later she sent me a picture of her sock stuck to an icky juice splatter on the kitchen floor. That week, time with her hubby was more of priority than mopping the floor. YES! YES! YES!

It is hard to set aside the mommy duties and remember that we were sexy, attractive, romantic people who adored our partners before kids came around. Hey, you still are all these things! You and your partner just have to make time for one another. It is good for you and for your relationship. Schedule sex if necessary. Set a bedtime for yourselves. Our kids know we go to our room at 10 p.m. We tell them "Don't bother us unless you are on fire, or your brother is on fire."

We have our own fires to ignite! Chores can wait. It's all about making choices.

Get Your Priorities in Order

Think of the level as a symbol for prioritizing. We cannot ignore the roles we play in life, nor should we want to. Like I said before, it's our relationships that give us purpose and joy. We just have to be careful that the "purpose" doesn't become for us to do everything for everyone else. When we prioritize, we send a message about what is worthy of time and energy in that given moment. I think that is what scares people about prioritizing — making tough choices. Choosing A means we can't do B.

Admit it, we don't like how some choices make us feel. If you choose to spend time helping a sick friend instead of going to your son's soccer game, you think your kid will think that you don't care about him. Really? Yes. I have heard parents say such things. Remember the last 12 games where you sat on the sidelines watching. You get credit for that. The reality is that if you go help the friend or even just grab lunch with the girls, the kids will see you have a life of your own. Maybe they will see a happier, more relaxed you because you come home feeling fulfilled in other ways. If you miss his game-winning goal, it's not the end of the world, his or yours!

Yet, do we judge ourselves and others for stuff like this? Of course, I feel badly for the kid whose parent is forever absent, but good parenting is not measured by a zero-absence policy. Look, this is not the World Cup Championship we're talking about. Of course, you want to support your child, but you can be a great parent even if you miss a few games, recitals, or classroom parties! I told my boys when I started working to build this business that I may not make it to as many sporting events as I used to. I told them to remember that *the depth of my love is not to be measured by how many games I get to because my love for them is immeasurable!* Moms and dads need to accept that perfect attendance is not mandatory. Go on the field trip if you can, but stop going on guilt trips.

And the Winner Is...

Making choices doesn't always mean that there must be a winner or a loser. Yes, it sucks when we make a choice, and someone feels like they lost. It makes for tricky family dynamics. I get it. Which side of the family do you see on Christmas; who will be left out? If we raise our kids in one faith, the other side will be upset. Tough choices remind us we can't please everyone. Who said we had to?

Did you ever hear the expression, "You can't ride two horses with one ass"? A lot of us sure try. This idea of making choices is a good lesson to share with our kids. They can't have everything, do everything, and be everything any more than we can. They can't participate in baseball and soccer and cross country in the same season. They don't want to choose. They want to do it all. (Sometimes it's the parent that wants them to do it all, and that's really not good.) When we make conscious choices, amazing things happen. We give the task our focused attention and it shows. If we do a bunch of things half-assed, we just eke by. In other words, if you try to put one butt on two different horses, you will fall off and I bet one if not both horses will run away!

Accept that some days you have to say "no" to things, "no" or "wait" to your family, your boss, your church, and your whatever. You have to say "no" because you are trying to find some balance, some sanity in your world. There's no need for perfection, just a semblance of balance that you can live with; one that is free of guilt and stress. Be okay with your decision to put yourself at the top of the priority list every now and then. Remember the airplane safety demonstration: Put on your oxygen mask first, then help others around you.

An article from Mental Health America sums it perfectly:

> With so many of us torn between juggling heavy workloads, managing relationships and family responsibilities, and squeezing in outside interests, it's no surprise that more than one in four Americans describe themselves as "super stressed." And that's not balanced—or healthy….Over time, stress also weakens our immune systems, and makes us susceptible to a variety of ailments from colds to backaches to heart disease. The newest research shows that chronic stress can actually double our risk of having a heart attack. That statistic alone is enough to raise your blood pressure!

There is no escaping the notion that we have lots of roles and duties in our lives but those relationships and responsibilities are not meant to be fixed to the wall like a shelf. You can't set a level on your life and expect it to balance out every day. Your life is fluid, dynamic, and changing, like a seesaw. Sometimes up and sometimes down. You have two choices. Make yourself crazy trying to keep that seesaw steady in the middle of the air or ride it out and laugh out loud when your ass hits the ground. I say, take some Advil for your sore bum and know that you will grow a lot as a person in the process of saying "NO!" Because you get to be in control, maybe for the first time in a long while.

Let go of your anxiety by saying "NO" to perfection, saying "NO" to being everything to everyone.

What can you do to better manage your responsibilities? What limits can you set? What do you need to say "no" or "wait" to? What do you want to make a higher priority? How can you make YOU more of a priority?

I will adjust my priorities…

As a parent by_____

As a partner by_____

As a child by_____

As a friend by_____

In business by_____

THE MONKEY WRENCH

You may be familiar with the expression, "Don't throw a monkey wrench into it!" It means something unexpected created an obstacle or problem. Well, I say let's look at those unexpected things as potentially *positive* events and turn this idea around. I want you to be a wrench! An adjustable wrench.

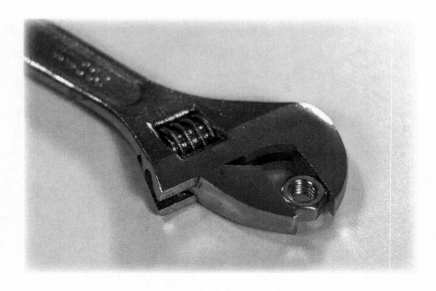

The adjustable wrench is a very versatile tool. Every home needs one. I use it on the kids' bikes, plumbing connections, and changing parts on other tools. Its key feature: it can handle lots of situations; it is open, flexible, and accommodating. Its sole job is to grab a hold of *nuts*. Yep, big ones, little ones, and in between ones. (I couldn't help myself. I have three sons and frankly, talking about nuts is just par for the course.) This wrench easily opens or closes to fit the size of the nut it needs to grab hold of. It can tackle your DIY needs and go with the flow.

In real life terms, I see us as the wrenches and those nuts as opportunities. Every day, we encounter the chance to do new things, to loosen up and turn things around. But do we act like the wrench: open, flexible and accommodating? Or are we rigid, inflexible, and closed off?

Carpe Diem

How do you seize the day? Do you grab it by the nuts or pass on the spontaneous moments in life? When I was younger, I played it safe. I was very passive and too shy to embrace a lot of situations with confidence — food, dating, and travel.

I grew up in an environment where we stuck to what we knew. The unknown was scary! I wouldn't even eat tomato sauce until I was 12. Plain buttered spaghetti for this kid. *Safe. Boring. Comfortable.* Does that resonate with you? Is that how your life feels some days?

It doesn't have to be. We can get past the comfort zone and be open to new things. It is ironic (or maybe not), but after I left home and had the emotional separation from my mom, I started to see the world in different ways. Things were less *scary*. In college and at work, I met people from different backgrounds than my suburban Catholic upbringing. I was open to the new perspectives and cultural differences I saw. Nothing good comes from isolating ourselves with the familiar. Had I not been open to going on a date with a Jewish guy, I would have missed out on the love of a lifetime.

What a lifetime it has been! My sense of adventure was tested when my husband was asked to work in Italy for 18 months. I agreed that six months was doable and I reluctantly set off on my first trip abroad — with our infant son and our golden retriever! I was frankly terrified. I had never left the East Coast, let alone considered a move to Europe. I gotta be honest, it was rough. Yes, call me a brat for saying this, but living in Italy was not all it was cracked up to be. We had major issues upon arrival like no working refrigerator, so I had to keep perishables on the porch for weeks. There were hundreds of dead stink bugs all over the apartment and the vacuum was broken. The elevator broke randomly so I walked five flights of steps many times a day rather than risk getting stuck in there with a baby and a dog!

It was no picnic, but my attitude was the biggest obstacle. I was very uncomfortable in my new surroundings and I put up roadblocks against every opportunity to really connect with the culture. I did not know much Italian, Ken worked 12 hours a day, and I felt like an outsider. So I stuck to myself and grew depressed after many long days relying on a baby and dog to keep me mentally stimulated. Neither was the best conversationalist. I counted the days until we could go home.

Now 20 years later, I have forgotten a lot of the lonely moments and remember the weekends when Ken, Matthew, and I would travel to Switzerland, France, and Northern Italy. We did make great memories as a family, but I regret that I did not immerse myself more in the experience. Beth at 48 is a much different person than Beth at 28. If I could tell that young woman something, it would be this: get out there and live. Don't let language barriers, metro schedules, and unfamiliar customs keep you sitting in an apartment feeling displaced. Suck up every bit of that magical adventure that others would have died to have. Don't be that insecure expat hibernating. Instead, be open to everything that life tosses your way in play, in work, and in love!

Play, Work, Love

Consider this scenario: Your girlfriend calls and asks you if you want to try a pole-dancing class tomorrow night. Oh, that could be risque, embarrassing, and physically hard to do. Do you say yes, not caring that you might fall on your butt and laugh yourself silly? Or do you give in to your insecurities of not being athletic or thin or sexy and use the old laundry excuse? Okay, if you are down to your very last pair of clean undies I get it, but honestly, why not be open to those playful moments when they pop up? The chance to do new things, even little things, is out there. It's what you make of those chances that matters, even if you get a callus on your hand from sliding down the pole. Dance, laugh, and throw caution to the wind.

When work throws you a nutty situation, grab on tight and go for the ride. I am so glad the 40-something Beth was more open to life than my Italian alter ego. Seven years ago, my business mentor, Jamie Broderick, called to ask me if I would be interested in going on the NBC10 Show, a Philly morning talk show. At that point, I had no ambitions for TV whatsoever. I had been interviewed on camera once before, but this was live TV. I remember pacing the kitchen as we talked. I would have three minutes to demo a few home repairs in front of a *live* studio audience.

Was I excited? Um, well, kind of. I guess. Honestly, my first thoughts were: what would I wear, who wants to hear from me, and would I look fat on TV? Sad, I know. That's where my head went, to a place of insecurity and angst. Can you relate? That day, something told me to take a deep breath and say, HELL, YES!

A few days later, I was at NBC studios. I was tossed into a green room, powdered up with some make-up, and plopped on a live set with Emmy-award-winning journalist, LuAnn Cahn. Any guess as to what prop I brought with me that day? A toilet, of course! (I should've had LuAnn autograph the lid because that toilet has been to many TV stations and stages since then. But now back to the program...)

I sailed through my segment, delivered all my points, and did not say anything stupid! I say this humbly, but I NAILED it! LuAnn said I was a natural. I loved my three minutes of fame. Not because I wanted to be on TV. Trust me, I still don't even like to watch the clips. But I love TV, YouTube, and video because media can be my tool to help others. These platforms allow me to reach more women, to help more homeowners. Now,

I have had over 100 TV appearances. I've been a guest on the Rachael Ray show and do live demos on QVC. National and regional companies have hired me for promotional and educational product videos. I produced a pilot for a DIY TV show of my own, *HIP Chicks Flips*. Nothing came of that show pitch *yet*, but that's okay. Other doors will open. When the right wrench and nut come together, it'll happen. Until then, I will remain open, looking for a nut to grasp.

Being open to new things can change the lives of the people you love, too. As I delved into TV and video, my son came along on the adventure with me. Matthew started making videos with me for my YouTube Channel when he was 13. After eight years, we have passed the two million view mark on our videos. Together, we became proficient in shooting and editing. And while I found my passion in teaching women, he found his in video production. He finished his master's degree in communication in Media, Film and Television. I am thrilled that my work experiences influenced him and opened a door to his future. Serendipity!

Hell, Yes

Life changes when you say, "YES!" I believe life begins when we step outside the comfort zone. I lived in the safety zone for a long time. My mentor Jamie once asked me to consider the things I was doing in my business life and to rate them according to how I felt about doing the same things in five years. My options for answers were "Hell, No," "Maybe," and "Hell, Yes." It was a life changing experience. I am glad I said, "Hell, Yes" to NBC!

Even as I began my business, I was stuck in fear. I worried if I was offering anything people wanted or needed, if I was knowledgeable enough to be taken seriously, and if I was attractive enough to hold media attention. In the last year, I realized that many people have gone before me and been successful in crazier endeavors. What made it happen for them? They were relentless, determined and did not quit. They didn't give a crap about the negative thoughts, insecurities, and obstacles (more on this in Chapter 9). Of course, most still had those feelings, but they didn't let them sit center stage in their head. They took the opportunities that came their way and made other ones happen. I am following suit, so I have flushed the negative energies away so I can be open, flexible, and accommodating! To quote Saturday Night Live's 1990s-character Stuart Smalley, "I'm good enough. I'm smart enough. And doggone it, people like me."

We can't let our fears and insecurities hold us back. What is your next "Hell, Yes" moment?

Making your profile on that dating site
Getting yourself in shape
Signing up for a dance class
Writing that book you think about
Applying for that job you really want
Quitting the job you hate
Traveling to a new place
Moving to a new city
Asking her to marry you
Asking him for a divorce
Making a romantic dinner plan for your spouse

Volunteering for a cause

Writing memories with your aging parent

Teaching your kid a skill

Starting a business

Becoming a mentor

I bet you have an idea of something new and cool you want to try. Write that bucket list. There may be some life-changing steps you want to take. Maybe you have something that has been tucked in the corner of your mind, simmering, just waiting for a sign. Here it is. Here is your sign!

Hell, Yes

What would your life be like if you were a little more like a wrench — adjustable, open, and accommodating? It is easy to look at others and see their missed opportunities. We all push our kids to live up to their potential, but are you living up to yours? Think of that nurse, Bonnie Ware, interviewing the dying patients. In their last days and hours, they shared the same fears that we have now in our younger lives. She says "Fear of change had them pretending to others, and to themselves, that they were content, when deep within, they longed to laugh properly and have silliness in their life again." They wish they had done something sooner to make their life different. Why wait?

Don't let today's fears become tomorrow's regrets.

Jumping into something new. Yes, that can bring on anxiety. It can also bring more fun, joy and opportunity than you ever expected. Just say, "YES." Yes to new adventures!

What are you going to do today, this week, or this month to be open minded, flexible, and accommodating to new opportunities? I'm not only talking about the ones that just come to you. Think about what you can do to create new experiences in your own life.

I will be more open…

As a parent by_____

As a partner by_____

As a child by_____

As a friend by_____

In business by_____

Safety Specs

For practical DIY purposes, safety glasses are an essential part of the tool box. Our sight is so important and worthy of solid protection. No one wants to lose an eye to a wayward projectile of tile or wood during a project. Our ability to see is a key part of our independence in life — driving, walking about, identifying hazards, and experiencing all the beauty the world has to offer.

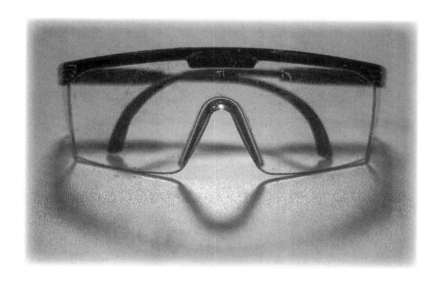

Why wouldn't we simply slip on a snug and secure barrier to safeguard it? That is the smart and safe thing to do when we anticipate potential hazards. We want to protect ourselves, right? So I ask you, do we need safety glasses for everyday life? I guess it all depends on how *you look at it. What you focus on!*

Our sight is the physiological image our brain sees and records in our memory, while vision is our perception of the world. How we choose to look at things is ultimately up to us. Of course, some things are very black and white and don't leave much room for interpretation or discourse. It is what it is. Other things are guided by *how* we see them. I believe the *how* is often based on how tightly we cling to our safety gear, that is *how much we focus on negativity and fear.*

No doubt, there are situations in life that require us to be guarded. There are moments in which we need to grab our proverbial "safety glasses" and wall ourselves off from danger. In the car, we fasten our seatbelts. We have GFI outlets in our house to protect against electrical shock. We don't swim without a lifeguard on duty. We understand the risk of injury or death from car accidents, shocks, or drowning. We are afraid it could happen to us or our family. Fear guides our actions to keep us safe. But being overly fearful can also drive us unhealthy and unhappy. We can obsess about every possible danger out there and not properly assess which hazards are a true risk to us in the given moment.

As I was writing this, we were in the midst of the CoronaVirus pandemic. It was day 31 of my family's stay-at-home order. This time has been filled with a lot of uncertainty and downright fear. I can't sugar coat this. Fear was driving all our behaviors. Fear of illness, job loss, isolation, and for many, a fear of death. We sat by the news watching the daily CNN death-count ticker as it climbed around the world and in our towns and cities. It has been very unsettling. We've wondered how we can protect ourselves. What does it take to stay safe beyond gloves, masks, and social distancing? We've felt trapped, yet knew that staying home would be our best defense. In this climate, our "safety glasses" have become six-foot-wide imaginary bubbles.

While we've sat in our homes awaiting the "all clear" declaration, we've faced great anxiety. Our lives have faced a new norm — and it is far from normal. It has been so easy to get caught up in the fear, especially when COVID-19 seemed to be the only thing covered by the media. Media overwhelm led many to a paralyzing sense of angst.

So how do you balance self-protection while maintaining your sanity? Like safety glasses in the tool box or N95 masks in the hospital, we have to control our risk. In this case, I'm talking about our emotional risk and vulnerability. Yes, the physical threat is there. But how do we manage the emotional risk of not *losing it* in unprecedented times? We have to monitor how much we expose ourselves to the reality of any unsettling situation. Our "safety glasses" may have to be substituted for ear plugs. It may be time to lessen the threat against our inner sanctuary by tuning out some of the rhetoric. The reality can be sobering and sad. We need to balance our information intake with our anxiety. Only you know what constitutes this balance for you.

Watching the news, especially in a crisis, can fuel anxiety. So decide on how you can best get the needed updates without getting sucked into the emotional triggers of the headlines. Pick a news channel to watch that seems less sensational or turn off the TV entirely. Spend less time scrolling the social media feeds and getting sucked into everyone else's fears too. Allow yourself just 15-30 minutes a day of news. Limit your exposure to toxic thoughts, people, and conversations. Carving out a peaceful space involves seeking to exercise control over what brings you negativity. It involves making a choice: focus on the positive, not the negative.

This applies to many things in life, not just viral pandemics.

Mr. Rogers so famously shared this quote from his mother, "When I was a boy and I would see scary things in the news, my mother would say to me, 'Look for the helpers. You will always find people who are helping.'"

Making a choice to look on the bright side is a powerful tool in and of itself. Over the years, many people have asked me how I kept a compassionate mindset toward my mom, one of forgiveness. I made a choice to focus on the good memories and not relive the bad. I focused on the fact that she was a good woman, I set aside her poor choices. I hung on to the moments of laughter, the holiday celebrations, the simple times we spent together as a family. Those moments still outweighed the unpleasant ones and I believe that is true of most relationships that fall apart. Love, joy, and fun brought you together long before the pain changed your perspective. I can tell you that that one mindset was a game changer. Trying to find the silver lining in every situation isn't always easy but it drives your focus toward solutions and healing and that ultimately helps you move forward with a clearer outlook and understanding.

On another perspective, the safety glasses can impede our vision at times. When I am working on a project in the wood shop, I keep my goggles on until the saw stops buzzing and I know wood chips aren't flying up anymore. It is then that I stop to take a look at what's happened with the wood! I can't always see the details of the cut as well with the glasses fogging my view. I may not like the reality of a crooked cut I just made, so I have to check. I have to come out from behind my protective gear, assess the situation and redo my plan. The same approach goes for life.

You, too, have to take off the protective gear or peek over the proverbial wall you've built to protect yourself. What's going on out there may be scary but if you don't fully see what's happening around you, you cannot act accordingly. Like my mom not wanting to go to a doctor because she feared she had health issues; not knowing the reality only adds to your anxiety and compounds the problem that's brewing in the first place. You need to be aware of potential dangers to the point that you can plan your next step. Hiding out won't prepare you. Sticking your head in the sand doesn't give you the upper hand over a bad situation. Knowledge will give you the opportunity to control your actions and reactions. Control brings calmness. That all comes from looking at things with both eyes open.

Just the Facts Ma'am, Just the Facts

In our world today, it seems like there are more and more threats we are told to be prepared for. The media, politics, and marketing platforms try to motivate our behaviors based on fear.

Remember this parental fear trigger — deadly Tide Pods? The real story is that foolish teenagers issued a social media challenge, daring others to suck on detergent packets. Only 86 cases were reported to Poison Control and no one died. This was not a danger to the general public. Yes, sadly some kids were sickened. But the media played it up because it was sensational, as pointed out in this 2018 article by Amelia Tait.

> Dr Sandra Leaton Gray, a senior lecturer in education at UCL and author of *Invisibly Blighted: The Digital Erosion of Childhood* argues these moral panics draw attention away from the real online issues affecting children and teens. "The issue that really ought to be talked about instead is the addictive nature of the internet," says Leaton Gray, who explains phenomena like the Tide Pod Challenge get more attention because they play on "people's worst fears" about endangered children.

This was not a threat brought on by Tide. This was not a public health crisis. It was the juvenile brain. We needed to focus more on what guides the poor decision making of youth rather than ways of locking up our laundry detergent. Yet the public was stirred up. The media successfully stirred the pot.

The headlines create fear. Fear drives viewership. Panic ensues. Fear cripples judgement.

From the onset of the CoronaVirus pandemic in 2020, we saw Chinese Americans targeted in the name of fear and hate. Uninformed folks blamed Chinese people for the virus and its origination. Restaurant owners, shopkeepers and public citizens became the face of the virus for those driven by fear. Some people were beaten, assaulted and verbally attacked. These American who happened to be of Asian descent had no more connection to COVID than anyone else. But fear drove people to fasten their safety goggles so tight that they couldn't see straight; they could not see the human beings before them. They let fear get in the way of judgement and moral behavior.

It is easy to do - let fear get in the way of judgement. Like I said, there are external influences that try to push us towards panic levels. When we are in a state of panic, our brains can't process information and we can mistake fake threats for real ones. Like I said before, safety glasses are a valuable tool but when they get fogged by fear, it is time to take them off so we can see clearly!

PPE

Emotionally, we all throw on Personal Protective Equipment (PPE) at some point. Sometimes, we hide behind masks so others don't see who we really are or we pretend to be the people others expect us to be. We wear gloves because we are afraid to get dirty and be all-in with our relationships — familial or romantic. We hide to avoid vulnerability. We are afraid of getting hurt because we got hurt before. I get it. Life is hard and we may feel safe hiding behind the gear, but living like that for a prolonged period only leads to isolation and sadness. We witnessed this during the Covid-19 quarantine. While we had to use PPE to stay physically safe, we were suffering from its mental and social implications. Putting the obvious health issues aside, we need to let ourselves be vulnerable from time to time, emotionally and spiritually.

When life's external stresses are mounting, it is important to teach our kids how to manage it. We show them best by example. It's okay to tell them how you feel. Share your fears. Let them know what worries you. Be vulnerable, but let them know you have hope. Let them know that you may not have all the answers but you are willing to ask the right questions, seek help, and do whatever it takes to move forward. Remember Maslow and his hierarchy of needs? He had this to say about fear:

One can go back toward safety or forward toward growth.
- Abraham H. Maslow

Showing our kids we are not going to hide behind the goggles all the time empowers them. It shows them the balance between fear and protection. You may need to fit them with some safety glasses of their own at some stage in life. There's no harm in that, but be sure to show them how to navigate without them. Show them when to step out from behind the gear and take control over the situation when they can.

For it is with clear vision that we can move forward! It starts being focused on the positive.

Take a moment to focus on your own behaviors. Do you let fear blind you from reality? Do you keep yourself so guarded that you can't fully live in the moment? There is a time and place to don those safety glasses. And just as importantly, there are moments when we need to be all in with eyes wide open!

I will look more deeply at the things that blind my perspective so I can face anything with a clear focus ...

As a parent by_____

As a partner by_____

As a child by_____

As a friend by_____

In business by_____

Duct Tape It

The saying goes, "If it is supposed to move and doesn't, use WD-40. If it is not supposed to move and does, use Duct Tape!" Because Duct Tape fixes everything.

What would an episode of MacGyver have been without duct tape? He could fix anything with a wad of gum, a paper clip, and some duct tape. If you younger folks don't know MacGuyver, Google him; he was the DIY Survival TV hero of the 80's, a problem solver extraordinaire.

Duct tape can solve many problems. As you see, it solves a big issue for me — it covers up my mouth!

Yes, my mouth. No, it's not a Catholic school punishment for cursing. If it is, I need to buy several rolls because I do have a potty mouth, but a few curse words are not as detrimental to our heart and soul as the negative things we say to ourselves. I slap that duct tape over the mouth of my inner naysayer. That negative, self-loathing voice in our head holds us back from being happy. It needs to be silenced.

(Please note: when I say duct tape your mouth, I mean it figuratively, of course. Duct tape on your face hurts, so don't do this at home! It's like a cheap hot waxing gone bad.)

We all have those harsh voices in our heads. Those voices that often began in childhood that tell us we are no good. These inner voices say things like "you're stupid, you're fat, you're ugly, you're old, you're not educated enough, you'll never get into that college," or the worst one — "no one will ever love you."

Sadly, for many of us, those comments are not just coming from inside our heads. They may have come from the very people who were supposed to protect us, inspire us, and elevate us: our parents, teachers, and friends.

It happens. Those people may or may not have known the power of their words. These words may have been thrust upon us as a criticism or chiding that was meant to motivate us or set us straight, but it hurt us instead. These words play over and over again in our heads, for days or decades, and eventually we believe them.

Almost everyone you know has a story of being shamed at some point in their life; a moment stuck on replay. A cruel nickname. A snide remark. A downright nasty insult. A discriminatory slur. Hurtful comments attacked our appearance, our heritage, our faith, our personality, our intellect, etc. The words so swiftly and carelessly flew out of the mouth of the sender and came crashing down on you like an atomic bomb. The initial blow was hard and strong, but the real damage came in the days, months, and years to follow. Just like toxic radiation lingers on the land, those painful words fester and grow in your soul like a cancer, slowly killing you and your sense of self-worth. Over time, we believe that what others have said about us is true.

Sometimes it is not just words but the behaviors of others towards us that chop away at our self-esteem. It is a combination of words and actions that most powerfully harm us. The pain of rejection is my greatest vulnerability. It hangs upon my neck like a stinky day-old fish. When you have gone through an emotional divorce like I did essentially (whether it is from a spouse or a parent or a child), a deep sense of worthlessness and rejection lingers. For me, it has been hanging around for almost 30 years. At this stage in my life, I have a fabulous husband, three wonderful and grounded sons, great friends, and a life's purpose I love, but the fear of rejection still rears its ugly head. At times I can't help but think that my own mother didn't love me enough to want me in her life, so why would anyone else?

It is an awful feeling.

I know many of you have the same emotions and have been through difficult times. Maybe you were adopted and wonder why your mother didn't keep you, despite knowing she believed she did what was best for you. Were you cheated on and lied to after years of devotion to your partner and you feel unlovable? Maybe it's your kids; you gave them the best you could, but they keep you at arm's length. Or is it that your family doesn't support your marriage, your faith, or your sexual orientation and that's left you feeling abandoned? You each have your own story. We all do.

This family stuff is hard; really hard. We all have some tale of estrangement and dysfunction. While some families really do put the fun in dysfunction and deal with it openly and loudly, most sweep it under the rug and hide it. I think we need to talk about it, not to disparage our family members, but to know we are not alone and learn how others dealt with similar dynamics.

If you don't deal with it — the self-hate and the depression — it becomes how you define yourself. And how you let others define you. The cruel voice inside your head only gets louder, harsher. I know how much these memories of disappointment and rejection hurt. Trust me, I get it.

Please remember this, I said it earlier, but it bears repeating:

My worth is not defined by someone else's
inability to love and respect me.

Please take it in. OWN IT.

You are worthy. You have incredible potential. You deserve unconditional love. Don't let anyone, especially your own inner voice, say otherwise. You will start believing it when you stop listening to the inner naysayer!

Getting Yourself on Your Side

This self-deprecation is a real issue. We also knock ourselves down over the everyday things. You know the horror of bathing suit shopping. How many mean things do we say to ourselves in that dressing room? "Oh my God, Look at my thighs, my blubber belly. I am so fat, so squishy. My boobs are droopy. This makes my ass look huge." Yeah, raise your hand if you have ever said any of that before. We do this, we focus on our flaws. I am guilty of this, too. Studying the crow's feet, counting the grays. I have put myself down and compared myself to other women, feeling inadequate.

Consider this: we tell *ourselves* things we would never say to another person. We would be horrible human beings if we said such things to someone else. We would be angry if our kids talked about themselves like we do about our own bodies. Then *why* do we tolerate us *talking about us* that way? Let's try being our own best friend, our own cheerleader, and our own biggest fan. It would be wonderful to always know you have someone in your court!

Now, are you done listening to that voice that says "NO" and "You suck"? It starts with slapping duct tape over the mouth of that nasty, mean-spirited inner pessimist.

Let's stop engaging in a volley of disparaging and self-deprecating words in our own head. The real world is harsh enough. In the past two years, I have been called chubby, weird, and old. I've also been told that if I were 25 and a bikini model, I'd get my own DIY TV show. I have had men tell me to go back into the kitchen and been called a hack. Did this stuff hurt? Yes, of course it did. But I won't let negativity rent space in my head anymore!

You deserve a safe haven away from the haters, the narcissists, and the painful memories. It's bad enough that we encounter hurtful people dumping their bitterness on us. We don't have to make it part of our story. Tell your inner critic to shut up and sit down! There just ain't enough room in your head for the two of you. Now is the time to write that eviction notice!

I have three exercises for you. One task is to respond to your DIY work below.

Your second assignment involves your tribe. Yes, you do have a tribe of folks who love you and think highly of you.

I want you to ask two friends or family members that have your back to do a little writing project with you. Do you remember creating acrostics in grade school? They are poems built around a word written vertically, in which each horizontal line describes the vertical word. Consider this example poem below. It's how you feel when you FLUSH the Fear.

Fearless
Lighthearted
Unique
Strong
Happy

Ask your two peeps (or more if you want) to email you an acrostic poem of your name listing the beauty, brains, and sass they see in you. Print that baby out and hang it up. Focusing on how others see you may be easier than believing the best in you. That is, until you start to see you like I see you. I think you are Fucking Fantastic!

The last task is a quick project. It's easy and no special skills are needed to make this simple tool for self-improvement.

Get an index card — the 3"x5" size is fine. Grab some duct tape. Put a piece of tape on it, a decent sized chunk to fill it left to right. Take this card and tuck it somewhere prominent, somewhere where you will see it often, like your bathroom mirror, car dashboard, office cubicle. or your refrigerator door.

Let it be a daily reminder to you that...

- you have the power to silence that negative voice.
- you can control how you think about yourself.

- you can stop saying mean things to YOU.
- you will treat yourself with kindness, praise, and love.
- you deserve unconditional love and it starts within.

Duct Tape is the tool to silence that negative voice. It will help you say "No!" to self-hate, and say "Yes!" to self-love. When you do this, you are more emotionally and mentally ready for whatever comes your way and your sense of self-worth is untouchable!

Let go of the fear of not being enough!

Say no to the negativity in your head. It's time to embrace and honor your body, your mind, and your heart. It is your time to shine and to love

YOU, all of you. Say something to yourself that is positive, encouraging, and supportive. Remind yourself that you are worthy and wonderful. Tell yourself how you ROCK…

As a parent by_____

As a partner by_____

As a child by_____

As a friend by_____

In business by_____

DRILL BABY DRILL

You have the power for self-improvement. We all do. The drill is a powerful reminder of our ability to change, not only ourselves but the world around us. Plus, the drill is simply my favorite tool. It is the most versatile tool that can be used as a drill or as a screwdriver. I mostly love that it is a power tool. Using one leaves you feeling powerful because power tools are loud, strong, and bring about change. They make things happen. They bore holes, cut things apart, and bind things together. They get things done.

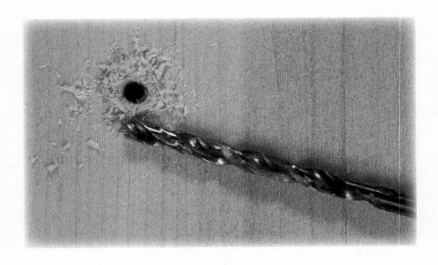

In my metaphorical toolbox, the drill can change lives. It helps us let go of the fear of not having a place in this world. It helps us create our own.

The drill is a tool for change. It takes a smooth piece of wood and bores a hole right on through. It makes a path, creating room for something new, maybe a nail, a hook or a dowel. With the right drill bit, you can make a hole for a doorknob in a slab of wood, and it becomes a door. Its work brings transformation.

The drill is an agent of change! And so are you.

Our lives are like that slab of wood, a blank canvas on which we can create something. We are the drill. We have the power to bore our own path in life, create something new for ourselves, and leave a lasting mark on the world!

I really believe in each person's power to bring about change. Good and bad. But let's focus on the positive. I know it's scary to initiate change. I was terrified to go out on my own at 21. I knew there was no going back. Could I live with that? I was afraid of not having enough money, of living alone, and of not having my parents behind me. Change is full of unknowns but as they say, our only constant in life is change.

I understand how my mom feared the changes before her. Changes in her health, the changes in her role, and the changes in me terrified her. Those changes were out of her control, or so she thought. She could have sought help with the menopause symptoms. She could have gone to therapy. She could have worked through this stuff. Her life could have been very different, but she was of another generation and mindset. It wasn't in the cards for my mom, but the help *you* need to make a change in your life is out there. You can take a different path and take back control when life sends unexpected diversions your way. We need to not resist it but learn how to grow from it.

Change makes us face the consequences. If this, then that? What if the change we make doesn't work out? It all goes back to that ever-so-common fear of failure. Yep. It's a big one! It holds us back from moving forward and taking risks.

Maybe you can relate. Perhaps you are afraid to quit your sucky job because you don't know if the next one will be any better. What if it becomes the best job you'll ever have? We get so worried about making the wrong change, about failing to do "the right thing" that we do *nothing*! For years. For decades. We get stuck, or dare I say again, *emotionally constipated*: paralyzed by fear, afraid of the unknown.

Here is a little lesson on fear and the physical effects it has on your body. Did you know that when fear sets it in, your colon shuts down? Your body enters the fight or flight mode and all its energies focus on survival; pooping is not a priority if you are being chased down by a grizzly bear. But you get the point, when we are caught up in fear, we can't let go of our crap. When we don't let go of our crap, we can't change. Life becomes stagnant.

While change comes easily for some, it is truly terrifying for others. And as unhappy as your current life situation might be, it is better than the unknown, right? Many of us have been stuck in that mindset of "better the devil you know than the one you don't."

We think that staying where we are will serve us better. We think staying in an unhappy marriage is okay; it's for the sake of the kids. We think we have no other options for employment, so we tolerate a bitchy *Devil Wears Prada* boss. We keep dating a person who we know isn't the love of our life because it's better than being alone and "Mr. Right" eventually walks away with some other chick.

We settle. We accept the status quo because we are afraid of change, afraid of the unknown.

Moving out of the comfort zone into the unknown is unsettling. We need to kick off the security blanket. You know the expression: "What doesn't kill you makes you stronger." This has been my mantra for a very long time. Embracing change not only makes you stronger, but also more empathetic, insightful, and forgiving. Our deepest, most meaningful personal development is driven by one constant — change.

Serenity Now

Ever since I was a child, I heard my father recite The Serenity Prayer. It was a favorite piece that he would toss my way when life got tough. Ironically, my brother, an English Professor, has spent years since my father's passing studying this prayer and is writing his second book about its origin and modern meaning. Most of us know it as the prayer associated with Alcoholics Anonymous. It is such a beautiful and powerful sentiment:

> God, grant me the serenity to accept the things I cannot change,
> The courage to change the things I can,
> And the wisdom to know the difference.
> —Reinhold Niebuhr

These powerful words give us pause to consider what we can influence and what we can't; when we should act and when we shouldn't. There are times when we can't change a situation. We can only change how we respond to it.

I learned I could not change my mom, I had to stop trying. I could not make her get the help she needed. I could not make her want to want it. Do you have a family member that you care about who needs to let go of an addiction or find a healthier lifestyle and you want it so badly for them, but they just don't want it for themselves? It brings a terrible feeling of helplessness. But we can't make others change. We can only adapt how we interact with them, pray they will want a different situation for themselves, and be there for them when they do.

Serenity in those moments is hard, but accepting the limits of our ability to bring change is important. It allows us to let go of the burdens that are not ours to carry in the first place. With a little wisdom, I figured out that I could not force mom to open the can of worms. It was her can, not mine.

The wisdom to know when to walk away and when to fight is not always apparent. We need to rely on our other tools to figure it out. The power of connection will help us. Connecting with other family members, coworkers, and mental health professionals gives us the insight, knowledge, and wisdom we may not have. It helps us decide how to act, if at all. We can't be expected to tackle change alone.

Being open, like a wrench, lets you consider new ideas to bring on change. Letting go of negative mindsets allows us to know that our desire for change is coming from a healthy place. Change driven by guilt, fear, and obligation will only end poorly. Change is most powerful and lasting if done for the right reasons and by the right means. Figuring out how to go about it can be the challenge and that's why we rely on our toolbox.

Be the Change

We have the ability to *influence* almost any situation in a positive or negative way. Of course, I suggest you find the most positive one. In those moments when life requires you to step up, to speak up and stand for something, you *do* have the power to make a difference. Do it with your vote, your words, your money, or your time. Do it for yourself, for your family, and for your community. Standing up to make the changes in your own life can begin a domino effect of positive transformations for everyone you touch.

Who doesn't want to leave a mark on the world? Maybe the impression you leave on the world today is a small one. You hold a door for a mom who is wrangling a few kids into Target. That simple act may mean nothing to you. To her, it avoided a major meltdown from happening when her twins, Jimmy and Joey, would have fought to hold it open and caused a scene like they did getting out of the car. What was a simple random act of kindness for you was a mood changer, day changer for her.

Perhaps the change you bring about has greater implications and affects more people. You decide to organize a 5k race in your town for a dog shelter. You create a sense of community, help the animals, and encourage healthy living. In the process, you do more than you likely realize. You set an example for others about community service. You teach your kids the meaning of collaboration. You inspire someone else to do a similar event in their town. You created a chain of good deeds. You never know where your acts of kindness will take others.

Take this to heart: when you act like a drill and you create space for change, you can change the world. Imagine that plank of wood again. Today, you might only have the strength to be a small drill bit and make a small impact. Next year, you may feel so empowered that you create a movement so big that you lead others to follow you on a new venture to a better LIFE!

The Do-Over

One of the things I like best about the drill analogy is that the drill has a reverse button. We need to be reminded in life that while there are some decisions and actions that are final, most choices can be revisited, big ones and small ones. Marriages sadly don't always work out. That dream job may become a nightmare. You might hate the couch potato to 5K training program. But there are other fish in the sea, and better bosses to be found and maybe you'll find that CrossFit lights your fire. Don't lock yourself into one option on your journey in moving past fear.

Life is full of decisions, choices, and diversions. I started my career in nursing. Look at me now. I'm a mom, DIY expert, contractor, speaker, author. I've taken a path far from nursing. Yet, my medical training and experiences are not wasted. The teaching skills I learned to educate patients about their health I now use to teach women how to care for their homes. Similar methodology. As a mom, I have had to wear that old nursing cap plenty of times caring for my own family. My problem-solving skills will never be obsolete. Knowledge is something that never loses its value.

Sometimes things don't work out how you'd expect them to or want them to. But the time spent in a relationship, a job, or on a hobby is never a waste, as long as you step back and look at the lessons you learned. The key is to change your course of action in relation to it. Growth from failure!

I do hate using the word failure but it's what most people understand. A win or a loss. Instead of looking at your next shortcoming as a failure, look at it as a lesson. Ask yourself, "What can I learn from this, for now and for the future?" It will take the sting out of the oops and help you make the needed shift with more grace and optimism. Remind yourself that the situation may have been a "fail" as my kids call it, but that does not mean that you are a failure.

So, in looking at the power of the drill and you as a change agent, it's time for you to step into your power. It's your turn to make a difference, in your own life and in that of others.

When I learned to stand up to my mom and fight for a healthy relationship, I had no idea that I would essentially fail in terms of holding onto family harmony. My family fell apart for many years. It was an unintended consequence for challenging the unhealthy dynamics. But a beautiful thing happened despite it. I set myself on a course of self-respect, self-discovery, and a lifetime of stronger mental health.

Changing the dialogue in a family unit is hard; sometimes you just can't. Resistance is just too high. You may only have one recourse: change yourself and how you react to the dynamics that bring you pain. Maybe in time, others will follow suit. As Ghandi famously said, "Be the change you want to see in the world."

That means you need to start by changing your own world first.

Say "no" to the status quo. Say "no" to the fear of change.

You are not too old to start over!

Get ready to change your world! What small steps can you take to influence others? What big changes are you ready to launch in your own life?

I will begin making changes...

As a parent _____

As a partner _____

As a child _____

As a friend _____

In business _____

11

THE STUD FINDER

The title of this chapter is not about finding the man of your dreams. I am certainly not giving out dating advice. In the DIY world, the stud finder is a tool to give you information. It has a simple function: to let you know where the wood framing studs are located inside your walls. This is crucial in renovation work. It tells you what's inside so you can confidently drill the hole or mount the shelf. You don't want to hang that

cabinet on a wall without a stud to support it, right? If you don't have the right facts, disaster may strike later when your work is not structurally sound, and your cabinet comes crashing down. The stud finder gives us insight on the things we cannot readily see ourselves.

In life, we need an array of stud finders to tell us what we don't yet know. They help us gather the information necessary for change and growth, be it personal or professional. Stud finders are simply a symbol for all the educational tools at our fingertips, because knowledge is our greatest tool for living a happier life.

Confucius said, "Real knowledge is to know the extent of one's ignorance." Wise words. Knowing what you *don't* know, is just as important as knowing what you do know. Admitting it is equally important. But if you are smart, you're willing to go out and get what you're missing. As a DIYer, I am always willing to admit what I don't yet know how to do. Even if I think I have a pretty good grasp of a project, I still research it before diving in. There may be another perspective that will just work better than mine. In everyday life, we really must do the same.

We all understand that knowledge is power. It moves nations forward. It breaks down walls. Heck, scientific knowledge took us to the moon! Knowledge is not limited though to the stuff we read in textbooks. More often than not, it's made up of life experiences — the wisdom we gain figuring things out for ourselves or learning vicariously watching others' lives unfold.

Some of the best life lessons will come from the screw ups, ours and everyone else's: the big ones, the little ones, and not-so-bad ones. There are times when watching someone else screw up is enough to make us think *I am not going to do what that doofus did.* But some of us—well, we've got to screw up a few more times before the lesson sticks! And that's okay.

To make solid life choices, we need more education and understanding about relationships, health, conflict resolution, and finances. These lessons are so rarely taught in the classroom. Sadly, it seems like it's not taught at home much either, because many folks don't know it enough to pass it on. It seems we often know more about calculus than we do about balancing a checkbook. These life-changing topics let us move forward positively, so we don't crumble when things get tough. Gaining good information about them brings security and an understanding of who we are. It enables us to function more independently and confidently in life. Having a better understanding of parenting, relationships, wealth, and health will get us through this crazy world. If we keep neglecting this stuff, our issues only get worse.

It's a shame that there is no state mandate on emotional, social, and mental health education before high school graduation. Our kids would be more prepared for independent living if there were. Conflict resolution, communication, self-expression, collaboration, and problem solving — these life skills are absent from most curriculum. Child behavioral experts cite the lack of problem-solving skills as a huge cause of anxiety, depression, and bad behavior in adolescents. They need to know how to navigate their world to feel secure in it. We all do.

When real life has us stuck between a rock and the proverbial hard place, what do we do? Often we give in to it, throw our hands in the air, or hide our heads in the sand. Please say "no" to giving up or running away. We have to figure a way out, just like MacGyver would have done. (And to think he didn't even have a smartphone!)

We need to teach our kids to problem solve, and need to challenge ourselves to do it, too. I think that's why I love the DIY approach so much. It forces you to think, to try, to readjust. We can teach kids by example. Learn something together. Knowledge is and will always be a source of power and control over a situation. When you know what to do, you aren't so afraid.

Today, we can learn the how-to's of almost anything. Thanks to technology, there's an app for that. We can take classes, watch YouTube, or read a book. We are so blessed in this country to have such access to education, whether it is from a college, the internet or the library. But how many of us take it for granted?

A lot of us do. Unfortunately, there are young Islamic girls in the Middle East who risk life and limb for the same education handed to us in the eighth grade. For that matter, there are kids in the most violent schools across the U.S. who drag themselves through drug infested neighborhoods to get to class. Why? Because they get it, they know knowledge is the way out. Knowledge can take them away from a bad situation and help put an end to the daily fear they face. I don't tolerate my kids saying, "I can't do it." It's a cop out. People with less means find a way to better themselves, so we can, too.

When my family life fell apart, I was a young woman who needed help. I turned to older adults I respected, I went to a therapist, and I read books. I did everything I could to work through it. I went out to find the direction, advice, and insight I needed. I gained clarity about my own feelings. I came to understand the psychology of the situation. And when I did, I could see my mom's perspective. I could understand how she felt watching her "baby" grow up and her role in life shift. I read about how menopause can change your mental state. I could understand that she was suffering, I did not understand then that she was suffering from mental illness, too. I came to that acceptance later. But I did learn then that neither one of us was at fault. I simply chose to work through it, and she did not.

I could look at the situation with my heart *and* my head. When we look at a situation only through the eyes of a broken heart, we see a distorted, shattered image of reality. An honest, objective view based on knowledge allows us to see the situation with a clear head so we can do the work we need to do.

Fully understanding a situation allows us to move past fear and act on facts. It is easy to get caught up in the angst of the unknown. We worry about terrorism, GMOs, global warming, and anything else the media tells us to. I am not saying these are not real concerns; they are. But too often the media thrives on making everything breaking-news bombshells. Fear drives ratings. When the media feeds us a spoonful of fear, step back and think it through. Resist the urge to get on the bandwagon if uninformed people are stirring the pot. I am always amazed how quickly people jump on that wagon without thinking for themselves. Some people do more research on their next cell phone purchase than they do on matters of health, relationships, and safety. If something worries you, investigate it. Find trusted resources and educate yourself. Make your own informed decision about how it might affect you and your family.

Wisdom, knowledge, insight — whatever you call it, it comes from inside and outside observations. We need to listen to both to figure out our own way and reach a healthy sense of self. In Maslow's Hierarchy of Needs, we reach that top level of self-actualization after we are fed, safe, loved, and affirmed. Self-actualized people are those lucky ones who are fulfilled and doing all they are capable of. They draw others toward the same state of mind.

Wouldn't the world be a beautiful place if we could live outside of fear and reach the top of that triangle? I honestly think we can learn to get there if we seek out the tools to do it. Read books, listen to podcasts, attend a seminar, better yourself anyway you can. You can still go deeper — deeper in knowing yourself and what you really need. See a therapist, meditate, do whatever it takes.

Getting to know yourself seems like a great place to start, right? Change and progress happens when we honestly know, like, and trust ourselves. When we know what we need to know, fear doesn't stand a chance.

Doing things on your own starts with learning how to do stuff. The resources you need are out there. What can you do today, this week, or this month to educate yourself? Be an Info Finder. Pick a topic. Try to learn more about a health concern. Listen to a parenting podcast. Read an article about retirement planning. Make yourself better informed so you can better handle life itself.

I want to learn more about X, Y, and Z

As a parent _____

As a partner _____

As a child _____

As a friend _____

In business _____

Measure Twice, Cut Once

We have all heard that expression at one time or another. I say it every time I do carpentry because it is easy to take a quick measurement and head to the saw. But it is even easier to walk ten steps and forget what you just measured. You have to measure twice, not only to confirm it's right, but also to have less of a chance of forgetting it moments later. A master carpenter may measure it right the first time, but the rest of us could benefit from a second view. Practice makes perfect, or at a minimum, practice prevents screw ups as we hone our skills and develop our expertise.

In my metaphorical language of tools, the measuring tape is a device for mastery, the combination of work ethic and skill to bring quality results. I don't really believe in perfection, it is a ridiculously high standard that causes us tremendous stress in its pursuit. Let's stick to excellence, proficiency, or best in show.

The tape measure represents our ability to work our asses off, overcome the odds, and get it done well. It's a symbol for our skills, the innate ones and the learned ones that help us conquer our inadequacies, because when you are the master, no one can steal your thunder.

Skill is about taking our knowledge and adding practice and perseverance to overcome nerves. Think about performers. Do you think Ed Sheeran is anxious before he takes the stage? You bet he is. More on him later. Most performers are nervous. My mentor says if you're nervous it means you give a damn. In moments like that, the anxiety is beneficial. You develop tunnel vision and focus on the task at hand. It pushes us to perform at our peak. Sometimes it leaves us shaking in our boots! Yet, anxiety doesn't have to overwhelm us as it drives us to do our best *if we are prepared.* Preparation yields mastery and mastery yields confidence; confidence kills fear!

There are many moments in our lives when we have performance anxiety. Think back to the driver's test. Oh, the nerves. Sheer fear rushed over you as that state trooper got in your car. You could barely choke out your name when asked. Wait. What? That wasn't you?

Maybe you were ready and calm. You gave it the practice it needed. You mastered parallel parking between the trash cans at home. You nailed the test on the first try! Good for you.

Me, I failed twice! Go ahead, laugh. I failed to come to a complete stop at the stop sign the first time and the second, I was too far from the curb when parallel parking. Third time's the charm and I let go of that blunder a long time ago.

In life today, with fake news and social media feeding us photoshopped lives, we can often feel inadequate and as inept as I did after my driving fails. We can look at others and think *I'll never be as good as they are at that. I can't ever achieve what they did.*

Don't measure yourself against others, especially those with fairy godmothers handing them an easy path to success, because you can't fight fairy tales. Focus your attention on the folks who took their raw talent and worked for it, whether job success, weight loss, or educational achievements. For anything you aim to do, study the people who overcame obstacles and follow their lead. They are the ones to emulate. They took tools to task and made things happen for themselves. You can, too.

Back to Ed Sheeran. He had to fight years of bullying for his stuttering, a lazy eye, and oversized glasses. At 14, he took to the road, playing as many as 300 gigs a year in random clubs. He'd sleep on park benches or in the subway, going hungry for days. He decided to post videos of his songs on social media and at age 19, he caught the eye of a producer who set things in motion. This ginger is now a beloved songwriter known around the world who worked his way past fear and obstacles to be who he was meant to be.

Just like Ed, we need to put in the work to be successful at things. Sometimes it could be our own family's interactions that we need to master. Communication skills are often harder to command than any sport or craft. I used to rehearse my thoughts before I spoke to my mom about sensitive things. I wanted to have my thoughts together, to feel prepared. Her emotions would skyrocket at times and I had to keep my cool while I tried to bring her energy down. I needed to express myself despite the rising tensions. I could say the same thing to her on two different days and get two very different reactions. Walking on eggshells is unsettling, so I practiced the conversation in my head, preparing myself for either reaction. Practicing what I needed to say was so helpful because I could be more focused on the goal of conversation and less distracted by my wandering thoughts if she pushed my buttons. This takes practice, but I found it gave me the self-control to keep potentially confrontational conversations calm. Less drama, less anxiety, better outcome.

This could be done with any interpersonal communication. We often proofread emails (or at least we should) before hitting send to make sure we have gotten our thoughts expressed clearly. Why not prepare ourselves for potentially difficult conversations? I don't want that to sound manipulative; it's simply a matter of thinking ahead. What is the goal of the conversation? Anticipate your response to the potential reactions. If you don't have your thoughts and feelings in order, you can feel thrown in front of the bus when dealing with challenging personalities. Been there, done that!

Whether it be a tough conversation, a competition, or a business presentation, you can better manage the everyday anxieties with practice, perseverance, and skill. You will feel more confident going in and if the outcome is not the one you desire, at least you won't feel like it flopped because you didn't do the work upfront. Preparation is not always a guarantee of outcome, but it helps avoid regret.

My husband often reminds me of the seven Ps: Proper prior planning prevents piss-poor performance. I love that line. I recently saw the seven Ps featured on a display at the National S.E.A.L. museum. The most well-trained, precise, skilled men in the world follow the seven Ps rule. Why shouldn't we? When we follow the seven Ps, we have less to fear, because getting past fear is a whole lot easier when we have our act together! Winging it in life is scary for most us and just yields more angst.

Even when you do follow the seven Ps, things can fall apart. Don't be afraid of coming up short at times. My driving test was a failure twice, even though I practiced a lot. I am now a fantastic parallel parker, even in Ireland on the wrong side of the road! Some of the greatest lessons we ever learn come from failing; that's how mastery is born. Call it a do-over or a Mulligan. Honing our skills teaches us to never give up and to keep excelling. When you have a setback, get back on the proverbial horse. Determination to get it right is the secret to success. Keep working at it until you are the master. The Master has nothing to fear!

How would it feel to be the expert in your own life — to be valued for your skills and assets, to feel more confident in general because you totally nailed one of the roles in your life? Mastery will empower you to squash fears as you stand in your powers. Whatever it is that moves you, don't settle for being the amateur in your own life. Be the expert.

Whether it be work, hobbies, personal growth, or relationship dynamics, end the cycle of insecurity. Do the work to own the skills you need to move the needle. Grab the big tape measure because you will need it to measure your progress. Practice yields mastery. Mastery yields confidence. Confidence kills fear!

This square represents a challenge for a lot of people. The fear of conflict is a biggie but it can be quelled by growing your confidence and practicing your delivery. Take time to know what you want to say and think about how best to say it with calmness and assurance. Practice on a friend before you share with your intended target. Accept feedback and practice again. Be prepared. Whether it is a tough family conversation, a business pitch, or a local contest for your favorite hobby, the seven Ps will have you handling life with more confidence. You can measure up successfully every time.

I want to master new skills in life to nail my role…

As a parent _____

As a partner _____

As a child _____

As a friend _____

In business _____

13

THE MOTHER OF ALL SAWS

Of all the tools I use in my arsenal, the table saw is THE tool I respect the most and for good reason. It's as loud as a lion, fast as lightning, and intimidating as hell. With its large jagged blade protruding from the deck, it's the ideal saw for cutting large pieces of wood, and fingers, too! It's a serious tool that requires proper focus and commands attention.

The table saw is a reminder of strength and confidence. It doesn't hesitate to tackle what lies before it. It is unapologetic in its power. It can chew things up and leave them in the dust. You can be like the saw. Tenacious, assertive and determined. You can put the power in power tool. You can be unstoppable, successful, and respected. You can be courageous. You can be a force to be reckoned with.

One time a few years ago, the saw kicked back and a piece of wood bounced into my leg, ripped my jeans and left a whopper of a bruise. It definitely gave me pause. Even after ten-plus years of tackling woodworking projects, I still feel anxious every time I flip the switch. But before I dive into cutting that plank, I fall back on my understanding of the saw and have trust in my basic skill set. I recognize the risks yet have a healthy sense of respect — a.k.a. fear. Does that fear hold me back from firing her up and getting shit done? Hell, no!

Why would it? I've been described as ballsy and bold, not just because I play with power tools or carry toilets on stage, but because I put myself out there. I lean in on the knowledge and skills I have gathered in life, in business, and in DIY. I use them to find my courage, to be like the saw itself and be my own source of strength.

You need gumption, folks. Call it bravery, balls, or chutzpah. Please know that things don't change without it. Truly moving past your fear and negativity starts with little victories of saying, "I can, I will, and I deserve it." What good is the knowledge you have or the skills you develop if you don't let them shine?

Do you remember the teacher asking a question and you knew the answer right away, but were too afraid to raise your hand? There are geniuses among us who have the answers, the inventions, and solutions to many problems, but if they live on the fringe, afraid to share their ideas. It is wasted talent. Yes, this next step is the hardest — putting it all on the line, putting ourselves out there.

Placing ourselves in a position for inspection and scrutiny is hard, especially with family. They tend to be the most judgmental of people, don't they? We are afraid of letting others see and critique what we have created and developed with our passion and energy. The risk of criticism is so unsettling that we would rather hold it back from the world. We can end up holding back our ideas, our goals, our desires, even our true identity.

Ask any creative type if they deal with this fear. How many brilliant artists never show their sketchbooks to anyone? How many beautiful novels are waiting to be written but the author is so afraid to pick up the pen? I get that one. You wonder, *Who wants to read what I wrote? What if people don't like it?* That's been real for me, but here we are.

I started this book idea a long time ago and have been dealing with that fear with every line I write. But it had to come out. Sadly, the courage came with my mom's passing. I was afraid my words would hurt her; that's the last thing I wanted. I feared everything I wrote would be misunderstood and manipulated. Nothing good would come of that, but I believed that my experience in surviving a deeply dysfunctional family situation could help others. Once she passed away, I found the strength to write as I worked through my grief, fixing Mom's house by day, crafting this story by night.

I stopped being afraid to revisit the pain of rejection, loss, and emptiness all over again. Telling the story with grace and compassion gives purpose to the pain by helping others find their own strength.

Finishing this book has not been easy. The triggers were there in the house and they were strong: letters she wrote me and never sent, a box of every card and photo I sent over 27 years' time, and the wedding invitation she declined. It was painful to face these reminders of the illness and lost time. Many days I came home in tears. I needed to be present in the pain to know that I was stronger than it. Owning the pain and doing the work of letting it go was exactly what I needed to do to find closure. I didn't know how badly I needed that. I realize now that I am stronger for standing in my fear.

Courage comes from believing in what's right and kind and healthy and believing in YOU!

I can't think of any other character that depicts courage more than the Cowardly Lion. This lovable yet cowardly cat is my favorite fictional character of all time. Ironically, he was my dad's favorite, too. We watched the movie together every year. It was an event with freshly made popcorn and my dad dramatically saying the lines along with the TV. Looking back, I only wish my dad could have followed the lion's footsteps and found his courage in confronting my mom to get the help she needed. But that's the trouble with mental illness, it weakens everyone involved, kind of like the poisoned poppies in the field that took hold of Dorothy and friends. Only in real life, there's no magic snow to break the spell of mental illness. That only happens in movies.

The Cowardly Lion reluctantly set off with his new friends on a journey into the unknown. This 'fraidy cat' saw the glory of meeting the wizard and freeing Dorothy of her nemesis. He wanted to stand in his role as King of the Forest and be who he was meant to be, but he was afraid of his own tail, not to mention his other concerns. He was afraid of confrontation. He was afraid of not being liked. He was afraid of the unknown! He felt desperately in need of a change and even wept about it.

Do you ever feel like that? I know I have. Standing up to my mom and standing up for myself was the most difficult thing I have ever done. It was also the bravest, most loving thing I ever did for myself.

Despite his shaking fear, the lion trekked thru that enchanted forest, escaped flying monkeys, and braved the Wicked Witch of the West. He faced confrontation, insults, and the unknown; everything he was afraid of happened. Although he didn't see his own bravery yet, he was *willing to ask for help* in getting where he wanted to go. Maybe that was his most courageous act of all. But as he stood before the wizard asking for courage to be bestowed upon him, the wizard replied, "As for you, my fine friend. You are under the unfortunate delusion that simply because you run away from danger, you have no courage. You're confusing courage with wisdom!"

Because...

Courage is not the absence of fear, but the ability to keep going in spite of it.
Courage is saying "YES," when that voice in your head says "No."
Courage is doing the right thing even when it hurts.
ourage is making the unpopular decision.
age is choosing when to act and when to show restraint.

Courage is standing behind what you believe in.
Courage is believing in yourself.

What you need to know is this — just like the Cowardly Lion carried courage during his journey, so do *you*. You simply forget what you have already lived through: cancer, addiction, divorce, loss of a spouse, and heaven forbid, the loss of a child. You all have something that you lived through so far. You keep getting up and living. You are ballsy! You earn that badge of honor every single day.

What gets in our way too often is that voice in our head that frightens us. That voice is a lot like the Wizard, trying to intimidate Dorothy and friends with his smoke and mirrors. Remember the line that was said after the Wizard was exposed to be a man and no wizard at all. He said this about himself: "Pay no attention to the man behind the curtain." The jig was up. That fake persona was no more powerful than the lion. The same can be said about the false perception we have of ourselves. It has no power over us unless we let it. We, too, have to ignore that voice, that imposter in our head that tries to diminish us. Step out from behind the curtain and remember this.

You show courage every time you…
stand up for yourself,
say "no" to things that don't feel right,
say, "I want more in life,"
work hard for what you want,
are open to new opportunities,
say "YES" to love
and when you say "NO" to fear.

Being bold and brave starts with feeling differently but it ends with taking action. Courage is just the tool that moves you to make changes; changes in the way you act, the way you think, and the way you show up in the world. Feeling ballsy is one thing, acting on it is another. Like when I was asked to go on the NBC show. I hesitated. I had to use a few of the tools in my toolbox to move me: duct tape to silence my inner naysayer, a wrench to be open to something new, a hammer to connect with the crew so I'd be invited back (and I was). I especially had to use the table saw, fiercely cutting through the crap that was holding me back. I did, and it changed my life. That day at NBC, I found my passion in using media to educate others. You can use the same tools to change your life.

Let me hear you ROAR!

Forget flying monkeys, fireballs, and freaky guardsmen. If the Cowardly Lion could push past them, you can push past your fear of failure. You've got your toolbox packed and ready to use. It's time to be ballsy and bold and courageous! It's your time to FLY.

Fear of
Failure

What can you do today, this week, or this month to find your courage? Who can be your guide? What small hurdle can you tackle to be braver? What is that one big thing you wish you could show the world about yourself?

I want to be more courageous and take action…

As a parent _____

As a partner _____

As a child _____

As a friend _____

In business _____

Part Three

My ~~Dootie~~ Duty is Done

I have led you on a journey to overcome fear, anxiety, and negativity. You have tools at your fingertips. They are in your personal toolbox; they have always been there. They just got a little rusty. Use them to conquer the negativity so you can move forward into the life you want to live.

Hammer — Use the power of connection to build your tribe, find support, get advice, or just remind yourself that you are not alone. Let others in; let others help. My life changed when I shared my story, when I asked for help. Don't suffer in silence. Fear fades when you have people who get you, get your challenges, and push you to a new stage in life. There is strength in numbers. Don't go it alone. Be a hammer that builds deep lasting bonds with people who will walk beside you.

Anvil — Negative relationships leave us living in fear and walking on eggshells. Fear and anxiety thrive waiting for the next painful interaction. I've been there. Use the anvil as a symbol of what not to be. You are not a pounding block. Not a doormat. Not the outlet for someone else's unhappiness. Stand up for yourself. Stand up to negativity. You deserve unconditional love free of guilt, pain, violence, or manipulation. Accept nothing less.

Wrench — Be open, be flexible, and be accommodating. Grab hold of the opportunities that come your way. Life begins when we move out of the comfort zone. Start small — take that dance class. Go on that trip. Take

134

that new job. When you get comfortable being uncomfortable, you find your passions and can tackle bigger goals as your confidence grows. Fear shrinks when you say "Hell, Yes" and start living!

Level — Anxieties rise when we spread ourselves too thin, when we juggle more than we can handle. Finding balance means saying "no" to some things and "yes" to others when it is right for us and for our families. It means accepting and embracing the imperfection in our lives. Anxiety doesn't stand a chance when you are at peace with that.

Safety Glasses — Seeing things in life clearly and wholly is important, whether those things are people, events, or situations. Our perception can often become jaded due to the past or outside influences, which may seem hard to overcome but it's possible when you can take control of how you look at things. There is a time to be guarded and a time to be vulnerable. Knowing when to be which is a life lesson that comes from focusing on reality, weighing risk, and deciding what is best for you and your family.

Duct Tape — Fear feeds off the voice in our head that says we are not pretty, thin, smart, or lovable. Your insecurities can stop you in your tracks. Slap some tape on the mouth of that negative voice. Shut her up! Hang your index card as a reminder to speak to yourself with kindness and love. You won't be held back by the naysayer. You are beautiful, capable, and loveable. You are enough!

Drill — Change is scary. Change is inevitable. Change is good. When fear has you stuck, change is the cure, no matter how small. If your weight keeps you from living your best life and you have 100 pounds to lose, set a goal for 10. Change one thing in your diet. Change one routine to boost your activity. Whatever changes you need to make, remember that no one is expected to change overnight. It's a process and you have the power to achieve meaningful change for yourself and for others. Change yourself, change the world!

Stud Finder — Maya Angelou sums this tool up beautifully. "I did then what I knew how to do. Now that I know better, I do better." Let the stud finder be a symbol of learning, of asking questions, and satisfying your curiosity. Knowledge is a key ingredient for change. Set yourself up for experiences that open your mind and challenge your established ways of thinking. Having new perspectives and insights allows for open dialogue and that can lead to open minds and hearts. Try this: pick one topic a week to learn more about. Google it. Read a book. Listen to a podcast. Commit to learning five new facts on every topic. Share them with others if you are so moved. But educate yourself any way and every way you can so you can live a better life, by doing better now that you know better.

Measuring Tape — Mastery, hard work, skills — this is what the tape measure represents. When we do the work, we see results. Whether it is a lifestyle change, relationship dynamics, or a talent, we need to keep working until we beat the odds. There are many instances in life where we have to practice, practice, practice. Sometimes it is a task that comes easily to us that we wish to perfect, but it's those skills that are not innate that require the most out of us. We fail and struggle to keep going. We question our ability to succeed. We forget that even master carpenters measure twice before they nail it, or should I say cut it. Don't let fears of inadequacy drive you away from the challenge. With preparation, perspiration, and perseverance, you will always measure up!

Table Saw — The mother of all saws will help you cut through your crap. It rips through fear and leaves the dust of doubt behind. Don't forget that you are fierce and powerful and worthy of respect. You have the power to make the changes you want to see in your life. Don't let fear and fake personas distract you from being the King of the Forest or The Queen of The Castle. You can live life on your terms being bold, ballsy, and brave!

Putting It All Together

All these tools work best when you use them together to tackle your project (that project is you). If you aren't sure how to do something, research it. There is no excuse anymore. Help is out there. Google it, take an online class, find a community workshop. If you need to be better at something to bring about the life change you want, practice. Make yourself a priority and do the work you need to do. It's okay if life gets a little unbalanced in the process. Keep your eyes on the goal — a happier, more confident you.

I have thrown a lot of ideas at you and given you a lot to think about. I hope it touched you in meaningful ways. I hope you act on the insight you gained. Remember, actions speak louder than words or thoughts!

I do believe that the most important tool for Flushing the Fear is the Courage, a.k.a. balls, guts, chutzpah. I know this is the hardest piece of the puzzle. The knots in your stomach, the tension in your neck, the stress in your mind: it is real. Fear of change. Fear of something new. Fear of the unknown. It can be paralyzing, but nothing is worse than living a life in pain and sadness, longing for something more. You don't have to anymore. You have the courage to let go of fear because you have done it before in countless ways. You have been packing the right tools all the time! You just have to open the toolbox.

I have told you about the tools I have used to tackle my own anxieties. One thing I have not done yet is share my deepest fear. I have had many challenges in my life, as have you. The greatest one, of course, is dealing with the estrangement from my mother. But my biggest fear involves the other person who has most influenced my life — my husband.

My husband is my biggest fan, my best friend, and the love of my life. Since we met, he has been the wind beneath my wings. I am very blessed. He has supported me in so many ways over the years. I want to support him, emotionally and financially. I want him to have the chance to pursue his dreams, like he has let me chase mine. My goal is to build my business, HIP CHICKS, into a national brand and have my husband retire from his work so we can run our company together! He shares this goal, too. Together, we want to create a family-based charity that supports women homeowners with home improvement resources and offers parenting education and life skills in low-income neighborhoods. A bright future starts with a loving and safe home. Our core focus will be changing lives for the better.

My greatest fear: Not meeting that goal and not being able to provide for him the way he has for me and our boys. I am working my ass off to make it come to fruition. I keep moving forward despite my own fears, so I guess you gotta stay connected to see what happens. But for now...

I Gotta Go

It's time to head back to the bathroom. My parting words to you are about coming clean with yourself. Go get that toilet paper and a pen! (Seriously, get up and get some TP.) You might feel like you need a whole roll right now, but writing it all out at once may be a little overwhelming. I want you to think about the one big thing that is holding you back right now. It can be a fear, an anxiety, or a self-deprecating thought.

Over the past few years, people have shared hundreds of squares with me, listing some very BIG issues and lots of smaller hurdles. Issues of family, work, health, and wealth. We all have them. We need to identify those things that overwhelm us and turn the angst into action. Right now, focus on the one issue that really has you stuck. It may require baby steps to part with it. It may need bold and swift action. One day at a time, one problem at a time. Prioritize. What can you handle this week, this month? Be honest with yourself.

Find a quiet space to be alone in your home, where no one is watching. It's time to let it go.

Cry, dream, grieve, hope, laugh, stand tall, but be sure to breathe.

Write down your fear. Focus on the letters as you go.

Let it out. Separate it from your soul.

It may be a part of you, but it does not define you.

Let the words fall out of your mouth as you read it aloud.

Own it as you get ready to release it.

This is your pain. It is real.

It is not stronger than you.

You can be free of it.

Walk over and stand in front of the toilet.

Look at your fear one last time. Read it aloud again.

You are bigger than it.

Know that you have the knowledge, the skill and the guts to move past it.

Trust that you are smart and capable and confident!

Tell yourself you deserve to be happy.

Now, boldly and bravely

Flush your fear goodbye!

Acknowledgments

All the great things in my life have involved my husband, Ken. This was no exception. For his patience and love as I wandered through phases and stages of healing and writing, I will forever be grateful and honored to be your wife.

For my sons, Matthew, Ryan and Kevin, who have made my role as mom the most beautiful, fulfilling experience of my life. For Matthew, who was my creative soundboard and partner in last minute crazy content ideas. I am forever blessed by my three sons!

My parents, Tom and Betty, for the moments that made me the strong woman I am today. I loved you then, I love you today and I will continue to do so until we meet again.

My brother Bill and sister Donna, whom I love more now than when we were kids. You understood I desperately tried to mend our family and always gave me a lifeline to stay connected (or should I say a hammer). I thank Donna for her genius and skill in graphic design for the covers and chapter breaks.

My other parents, Stan and Marlene, who are so much more than in-laws and rose up as Mom and Dad in every sense.

My beloved aunts, Rosemary and Gerry, who have been both friends and confidantes through the years and have always welcomed me and my family to the holiday table.

My sister-in-law, Emilia for quietly propping me up and sharing in the renovation of Mom's house and my heart.

Denice Whiteley, my faithful assistant, who has the ever-challenging role of keeping me focused and on task. Thanks for the laughter and tears through the years. You are my left brain.

Brigitte Rogers, my friend and cheerleader who believed in me and this message before I fully did.

Pam Scott, Sue Bokmuller, and Amy Murphy, lifelong friends, who held my hand through the hardest moments as I lost my mom back in the day.

Sharon and Frank Cerauli and Maureen Larsson, dear friends, for having my back as I grieved losing my mom for the second and final time.

Kate Hambly, for pointing me to the perfect gift for myself — the Hammer Home Your Message necklace that I wear proudly. It helped me nail the last stages of this book with courage.

Kara Raudenbush and Danielle Soloff, my talented photographers, for capturing both my sass and my soul, with artful expression.

Mary Fran Bontempo, for her guidance and example in writing from the heart and telling my story unapologetically.

Julie Singer for her unending support and the gift of the perfect TP for ghost writing the toilet paper confessions.

Jamie Broderick, my mentor, for making me cry in Starbucks the day I said "Hell, Yes" to my future goals. It was a life changing moment.

Michael Port, my mentor, who told me to share this story without reservation and reminded me to never water myself down. Mission accomplished.

Laurel Garver, my editor and button pusher, for making me go deeper in order to create a more meaningful message and for trying to keep it less "potty mouthed."

Dr. Appelstein, whose gentle words and sincere concern for a young woman were life changing.

Nella, my golden retriever, who kept my lap warm and my heart happy as I finished this book.

References

Part One: Flushing Fear

"Anxiety and Physical Illness." Harvard Health Publishing.
9 May 2018, https://www.health.harvard.edu/staying-healthy/
anxiety_and_physical_illness

Chapter 1. Where Does The Crap Come From?

Amodeo, John, "Deconstructing the Fear of Rejection," Psychology
Today, 4 April 2014, https://www.psychologytoday.com/us/
blog/intimacy-path-toward-spirituality/201404/deconstructing-
the-fear-rejection.

Cohut, Maria. "Death anxiety: The fear that drives us." Medical
News Today, 11 August 2017, https://www.medicalnewstoday.
com/articles/318895.php#7

"How to Overcome Fear of Poverty," Uncommon Knowledge, https://
www.hypnosisdownloads.com/fears-phobias/fear-poverty

Vilhauer, Jennice, "Why the Fear of Disappointment Is Detrimental
to Your Life," Psychology Today, 27 September 2017, https://
www.psychologytoday.com/us/blog/living-forward/201709/why-
the-fear-disappointment-is-detrimental-your-life

Winch, Guy, "10 Signs That You Might Have Fear of Failure."
Psychology Today, 18 June 2013, https://www.psychologytoday.
com/us/blog/the-squeaky-wheel/201306/10-signs-you-might-
have-fear-failure

Chapter 4. It's Hammer Time
"Intimacy vs. Isolation: Psychosocial Stage 6," VeryWell Mind,
9 November 2019, https://www.verywellmind.com/intimacy-
versus-isolation-2795739.

Mcleod, Saul, "Maslow's Hierarchy of Needs," Simply Psychology,
20 March 2020, https://www.simplypsychology.org/maslow.html

Chapter 5. The Acme Anvil
"Narcissistic Personality Disorder," Psychology Today,
7 February 2019, https://www.psychologytoday.com/us/conditions/
narcissistic-personality-disorder

Chapter 6. I Gotta Level With You
"Work Life Balance," Mental Health America, https://www.
mhanational. org/work-life-balance

Chapter 8. Safety Specs
Tait, Amelia, "Only 86 Teens Ate Tide Pods, So Why Did the World
Erupt in Moral Panic?" NewStatesman, 30 January 2018, https://
www.newstatesman.com/science-tech/internet/2018/01/only-86-
teens-ate-tide-pods-so-why-did-world-erupt-moral-panic

Made in the USA
Columbia, SC
10 July 2020